Inferno

The Great Boston Fire of 1872

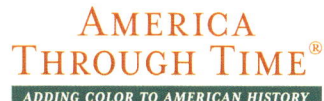

For the Whites
with best wishes
Anthony M Sammarco

ANTHONY M. SAMMARCO

AMERICA
THROUGH TIME®
ADDING COLOR TO AMERICAN HISTORY

This book is dedicated to the heroic firemen who
lost their lives fighting the Great Boston Fire

Albert Abbott, Lewis Abbott, Daniel Cochrane, John Connelly, William Farry, William Frazier,
Thomas Maloney, Frank Olmstead, Henry Rogers, Martin Turnbull, Walter Twombley;
and two volunteer firefighters Michael Fitzgerald and Lewis Thompson

Bravely and skillfully did the firemen fight the foe which had dealt them such hard blows

America Through Time is an imprint of Fonthill Media LLC
www.through-time.com
office@through-time.com

Published by Arcadia Publishing by arrangement with Fonthill Media LLC
For all general information, please contact Arcadia Publishing:
Telephone: 843-853-2070
Fax: 843-853-0044
E-mail: sales@arcadiapublishing.com
For customer service and orders:
Toll-Free 1-888-313-2665

www.arcadiapublishing.com

First published 2022

Copyright © Anthony M. Sammarco 2022

ISBN 978-1-63499-423-1

Typeset in Mrs Eaves XL Serif Narrow
Printed and bound in England

CONTENTS

Fireman Augustus A. Lawrence was a
member of Bunker Hill Hose Co. 2, which was
located at 556 Main Street in Charlestown,
Massachusetts. He was one of many men who
fought the Great Boston Fire.

ACKNOWLEDGMENTS

I wish to extend my sincere thanks and deep appreciation to:

Boston Athenaeum, Christina Michelon; Boston Public Library, David Leonard; Boston City Archives; Boston Sparks Association; Box 52 Association; Pasqualina and Donato Cedmarco; Cesidio "Joe" Cedrone; Paul Christian, retired Boston Fire Chief; City of Boston, Michelle Wu, Mayor; Edie Clifford; Colortek, Jackie Anderson; Peter Cook; Coyle's Auction Inc., Nancy Wyman; Digital Commonwealth; Michael Doolin; eBay; Mary Ann English; Gibson House Museum, Samuel Hammond; Victoria Gall; Edward Gordon; Grand Lodge of Masons, Gerard Gilmore Jr., Grand Master; Josh Greenland; Dan Haacker; Helen Hannon; Historic New England, Lorna Condon; George Kalchev, Fonthill Media; Peter B. Kingman; Library of Congress; Kena Longabaugh; Massachusetts Historical Society; the late Frank Norton; Orchard House Museum, Jan Turnquist; Orleans Camera; the late Stephen D. Paine; Susan W. Paine; Panopticon Imaging, Paul Sneyd; William H. Pear, II; the late Jeanette Lithgow Peverly; Richard Rabbett; Lilian M. C. Randall; Miriam Rubinoff; Henry Scannell; Ron Scully; Robert Bayard Severy; Richard Sheaff; Skinner, Inc., Elizabeth Haff; Maureen Smith; the late Verity Carslile Smith; Alan Sutton, Fonthill Media; Jamie Sutton; Archives and Special Collections, University of Massachusetts, Sammarco Collection; Kenneth Turino and Chris Matthias; Captain John P. Vahey; Vose Galleries, Carey Vose; Waterworks Museum, Tracy Lindboe.

Royalties from the sale of this book will benefit the Boston Athenaeum, Sammarco Print Room Fund.

Photographs, unless otherwise credited, are from the collection of the Boston Public Library.

Introduction

This book, *Inferno: The Great Boston Fire of 1872*, was written to commemorate the 150th anniversary of a devastating fire that destroyed 65 acres of land in the city, from Washington Street, between Summer Street and Milk Street, fanning eastward towards the wharves projecting into Boston Harbor.

In the mid-nineteenth century, Boston was undergoing major changes through the topographical infilling of the South End on either side of "The Neck" of Boston, the massive infilling of the Back Bay marshes as well as the increase in population by matriculation and immigration. Following the Civil War, Boston was to see its population increase to 250,000 by 1870 of which one half was either immigrants or the children of immigrants. The city was embracing change, ethnic as well as religious, and was a far cry from the homogeneous town settled by the Puritans from England in 1630.

By 1872, much of the former residential neighborhood known as the South End had given way to commerce. Summer, Bedford, Kingston, Arch, Franklin, and Federal Streets and others had once been the pride of the Athens of America, but by the 1860s, most of its residents had moved to the newly filled South End, the Back Bay, and the suburbs. The area was rebuilt with impressive five-story commercial blocks that not only changed the face of Boston, but were architecturally impressive with "their splendid fronts" that became the pride of Victorian Boston, its merchants and the Bostonians who now thronged to the area.

However, these buildings, though built of granite and brick, had wood-framed Mansard roofs. Introduced to Boston in 1848 by Jean Lemoulnier who designed the Deacon House in Boston's South End, the Mansard or "French" roof was a popular feature of both residential and commercial buildings. It was the Klous Building, at the corner of Summer and Kingston Streets, where the fire began on Saturday evening November 9, 1872. The fire spread quickly for a number of reasons, not just the epizootic that laid low the horses who could not pull the fire engines, but the wood-framed Mansard roof provided combustible material for the fire and the narrow streets enabled the fire to spread quickly from one building to another and from street to street. The fire department struggled to fight the blaze due to different sized couplings for hoses to hydrants, as well as inadequate water pressure from the hydrants, which could not produce a water stream that could reach above the third story of the burning buildings. The low water pressure made it difficult to get water to the top floors and roofs of buildings. The fire spread rapidly and to try to stop the fire buildings were blown up to create a firebreak, which proved unsuccessful. Fire Chief John S. Damrell had been pressured by Mayor William Gaston, aldermen, and a council of concerned citizens to use explosives to destroy buildings that lay in the path of the spreading fire. This strategy failed as many buildings did not fall after the explosions that were meant to level them, and the fires that began as a result of the explosions may have allowed the spread of the fire beyond Federal and Milk Streets.

A chronology of the fire is as follows:

7:00 p.m., November 9: the fire begins in the basement of the Klous Building;

7:24 p.m., November 9: first alarm is received from Box 52 on Summer Street;

8:00 p.m., November 9: all twenty-one of Boston's fire engines are at the scene of the fire;

10:00 p.m., November 9: the fire spread to a three block radius from Summer Street northward;

12:00 a.m., November 10: the fire spread to a five block radius;

4:00 a.m., November 10: the fire spread to the waterfront, destroying wharves and docked boats;

4:00 a.m., November 10: gunpowder was used on Congress Street to create a fire block;

6:00 a.m., November 10: the fire reached Washington Street and spread through the center of downtown;

12:00 p.m., November 10: the fire is stopped and contained before it destroys the Old South Meeting House.

There are many stories associated with the heroism of the firemen and militia who fought the fire and protected the area, but one poignant story is that of Rosamond Warren Gibson who lived at 137 Beacon Street in the Back Bay (now the Gibson House Museum). She had become so alarmed by the glaring light of the fire that she went to her parents' house at 2 Park Street to remove family heirlooms and bring them to her house, which was a distance from the fire. Among the family heirlooms saved was a large portrait of *Cleopatra Dissolving the Pearl*, a copy of a Titian by Guido Reni that Samuel Crowninshield had acquired on the Grand Tour of Europe. She recounted the harrowing event:

Many of the horses at that time were ill with epizootic but Lawrence Curtis secured a Kenny & Clark hack and called in the middle of the night to take me up there.... On arriving, I found the silver, most of which consisted of my own wedding presents, in a large wooden and silver chest. This with other precious things, too large for the hack, was put in the cart, after having placed on top the picture of Cleopatra Dissolving the Pearl, by Guido Reni, a family heirloom from my Grandfather Crowninshield. Having secured all we could and the cart having been sent off, we started for home in the hack. Imagine my horror, on reaching the State House, to find Cleopatra lying in the road with the chest on top of her! It seemed that someone had run into the cart and upset it, and the horse, breaking away, had run back to the stable. Kind friends, however, came to the rescue, picked up the treasures, righted the cart, and dragged it to No. 137. There, to my despair, we found that the corner of the chest had gone through Cleopatra's hand, and I trembled to think what my mother would say. Fortunately, we had it beautifully restored, but as the fire never reached Park Street after all, the picture would have been much safer where it was.

Mrs. Gibson's plight was similar to many who sought to save things from the encroaching fire, but after the fire was quelled, many began to place the blame on the once fashionable Mansard roofs that had architecturally transformed Boston over the previous two decades. Reverend Cyrus Bartol said: "In the blackened remains yonder, we not only perceive human negligence, but decipher the name of God." Was it the negligence of architectural design, the lack of water power for buildings taller than the rowhouses they replaced, or negligence for zoning and building codes? Or could it possibly be a mélange of all three?

The fire was said to have destroyed 776 buildings in Boston's downtown, causing over $73 million (1872 dollars or $1,682,000,000.00 in 2022 dollars) in damage, killing an estimated twenty people and led to stricter building regulations in Boston. Fires have always been a constant source of anxiety, but this inferno was cataclysmic and beyond the comprehension of many people. The city of Boston took action and appointed a city architect that would oversee all building in the city. They also made resolutions:

> Resolved, That the citizens of Boston respectfully but earnestly request the commissioners of streets and city council of Boston immediately to revise and establish the lines of the streets in the district upon a comprehensive and liberal plan, relying on the character, energy, and progressive spirit of the people to approve such action; and we pledge ourselves to support the commissioners and city council in the exercise of the power and responsibility belonging to them in this regard.

> Resolved, That the citizens of Boston earnestly request the city council to prohibit any further construction of Mansard roofs, and to limit the height of all buildings within the city limits, so that such a conflagration as has just taken place may not be repeated.

> Resolved, That the appeal to the city of Boston to establish anew in the burnt district the lines of all the streets which are too narrow or too crooked for the present and future wants of the chief city of New England, imperatively demands immediate action.

> Resolved, That the time and opportunity for the erection of a Merchants' Exchange in the center of business, associating together all engaged in mercantile pursuits, has arrived; and we strongly advise that steps be taken at once to procure a charter from the legislature, to purchase a proper site, and to erect a suitable building adapted to the uses, and worthy, of the merchants of Boston.

On November 10, 1873, a ceremony commemorating the first anniversary of the fire was observed, with Frederick O. Prince, mayor of Boston, aldermen, and other city officials visiting the Burnt District to inspecting the improved and widened streets, impressive new buildings as well as those still under construction, all of which were to have roofs that were noncombustible. Within a decade, the area was rebuilt and was once again a destination.

Currier and Ives dramatically depicted *The Great Fire at Boston* as seen from Boston Harbor with excursion boats, ferries, sailboats, and rowboats filled with spectators watching the cataclysmic fire that would eventually destroy 65 acres of Downtown Boston. It was said that the "church steeples, and especially the dome of the State House, stood out in brilliant magnificence, while every street which centered upon the vast conflagration was radiant with the light of the great fire." (*Author's collection*)

1

BOSTON: THE ATHENS OF AMERICA

In 1822, Boston voters embraced a municipal form of government and henceforth was to be known as the city of Boston. An urbane, cultured, well-educated populace had long contributed to the city being viewed as an innovative leader in education, humanity and benevolence since the early nineteenth century and was referred to as the Athens of America. Seen here is Summer Street with the New South Church, referred to as the Octagonal Church, facing Church Green. Designed by Charles Bulfinch and built in 1814 of granite quarried in Chelmsford, it was flanked by Bedford and Summer Streets and was built in what was described as "the most beautiful avenue in Boston." (*Collection Massachusetts Historical Society*)

The Tontine Crescent was designed by Charles Bulfinch and built in 1795 on Franklin Place (now Street) between Washington and Federal Streets. On the north side of the street, facing the sixteen connected rowhouses with an impressive center pavilion, were duplex houses, of the same gray-painted brick and classical architectural details as those of the crescent. In the foreground was a fence enclosed tree-lined park in which Bulfinch had placed a large classical urn brought from Europe and set on a plinth base in memory of Benjamin Franklin, for whom the street was named. (*Author's collection*)

The residential quality of the neighborhood around Summer Street is evident by this photograph of the early 1860s with a corner of the portico of the Octagonal Church on the right and rowhouses on the left along Bedford Street leading to Chauncy Street. The wide expanse of the open square in the foreground, paved in cobblestones, created an impressive approach to the church and has long been known as Church Green. Samuel Adams Drake said: "Summer Street was, beyond dispute, the most beautiful avenue in Boston. Magnificent trees then skirted its entire length, overarching the driveway with interlacing branches, so that you walked or rode as within a grove in a light softened by the leafy screen of elms."

The Old South End

The Old South End of Boston was considered the epitome of urbane living in the early nineteenth century. Charles Bulfinch had introduced neoclassicism in the 1790s with the design of the Tontine Crescent on Franklin Place. In fact, Samuel Adams Drake, author of *Old landmarks and Historic Personages of Boston*, said: "Summer Street was, beyond dispute, the most beautiful avenue in Boston ... [shaded by] a grove in a light softened by the leafy screen, and over the shadows of the big elms lying across the pavement." The neighborhood also had numerous places of worship; the First Church of Boston, Trinity Church, Old South Meeting House, New South Church, the Federal Street Church, the Church (later Cathedral) of the Holy Cross, and the Church of the Savior were all within just a few blocks of one another and are testimony to the aspect of a neighborhood.

However, by the late 1850s, commercial development began to change the character of the area. Topographical development in Boston had only recently begun, with Beacon and Pemberton Hills leveled and the soil used to infill the Flat of Beacon Hill and the area of Causeway Street, respectively. In the 1850s, the infilling of the South End beyond Dover Street began in earnest, creating a residential area that stretched to the city of Roxbury. As Boston's population increased by both matriculation as well as by immigration, the area of Church Green was redeveloped and rowhouses were demolished. In fact, the New South Church was demolished in 1868 and replaced with a bank. Drake was poignant in stating "The palaces of trade now rear their splendid fronts where [once] stood the gardens or mansions of the old merchants or statesmen of Boston." In the 1860s, no longer the fashionable neighborhood of a decade before, the Old South End gave way to change with whole streets of granite commercial blocks replacing the refined rowhouses designed by Charles Bulfinch and Asher Benjamin.

Frank E. Frothingham said of the newly built-up area in the early 1870s: "In those lofty structures which graced Franklin, Summer, High Pearl, Federal, Congress, and Devonshire streets, were piled up the accumulated products of Lowell, Lawrence, Manchester, Lewiston, and other milling places, as well as the results of the labor of toiling thousands in the boot and shoe manufactories throughout the eastern portion of Massachusetts."

Avon Place was a short street that ran from Washington Street, opposite Temple Place, to Chauncy Street. Avon Place was once the home of Henry H. Fuller, a celebrated lawyer; Nathaniel Bradlee, father of the Reverend Caleb Davis Bradlee and Nathaniel J. Bradlee the architect; Charles White, the Washington Street druggist who sold the cure-all "Matchless Sanative" and Captain Hales Suter, a retired ship master. By the early 1860s, when much of the neighborhood had already become commercial, Avon Place was still a charming residential enclave with red brick rowhouses built in the early nineteenth century, which retained a certain charm.

Since the mid-eighteenth century, Summer Street had been one of the more fashionable residential areas in Boston. This duplex red brick Greek Revival rowhouse was designed by Asher Benjamin for Richard D. Tucker and James W. Paige. It had Ionic columns flanking the two entrances, swell-bay facades, fanciful carved window lintels, roof cresting, and impressive cast-iron balconies and fencing with superb urns. It faced Church Green and was indicative of the well-designed houses built in the 1830s. As the neighborhood changed, and became less desirable as a place of residence, this duplex house was demolished in 1865.

This three-story rowhouse was once the home of Daniel Webster and was at the corner of Summer and High Streets, facing Church Green. Webster was a great statesman who represented Massachusetts in the United States Congress and served as secretary of state under Presidents William Henry Harrison, John Tyler, and Millard Fillmore. The mansion later became the home of Peter Chardon Brooks, a wealthy merchant and president of the New England Insurance Company. Upon his death in 1849, Brooks was said to be Boston's first millionaire and one of the 100 wealthiest Americans of all time. The large number of trees and pleasant gardens gave this neighborhood a certain distinction.

The Old South Meeting House was designed by Robert Twelves and built in 1729 by Joshua Blanchard at the corner of Washington and Milk Streets. It was the second place of worship of the Third Congregational Church in Boston, which was gathered in 1669. After the Boston Massacre in 1770, annual meetings on the anniversary were held at the church until 1775, with John Hancock and Dr. Joseph Warren addressing the audience. In 1773, patriots met in the meeting house to debate British taxation without representation in parliament and, after the meeting, a group dressed as Mohawk Indians raided three tea ships anchored nearby in what became known as the Boston Tea Party. Saved by valiant efforts during the fire of 1872, it was later restored by the Old South Association in Boston and has today become an important part of the Boston Freedom Trail.

Chauncy Street, looking towards Summer Street, had the Chauncy Hall School, the headquarters of the Massachusetts Charitable Mechanics Association, and the First Church of Boston. Chauncy Hall School, a preparatory school, was founded by Gideon Thayer in 1828. The Massachusetts Charitable Mechanics Association, founded in 1795, was built in 1860 in the Italian Renaissance style, with Mechanics Hall on the third floor. The First Church was designed by Asher Benjamin and built in 1808 and is one of the oldest religious societies in Boston.

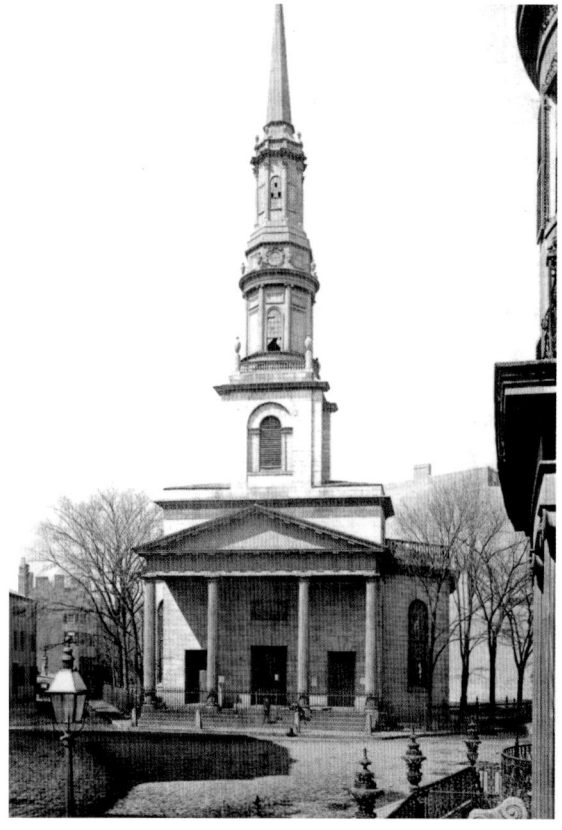

The New South Church, founded in 1714 and often referred to as the Octagonal Church, was designed by Charles Bulfinch and built in 1814 at Church Green, the junction of Summer Street, which curves towards the right, and Bedford Street. The church was built of Chelmsford granite and when completed in 1814, was in a neighborhood which was an upscale residential area. In 1868, the church merged with the New South Free Church as the neighborhood had become increasingly commercial; the New South Church was demolished in 1868 and replaced with a bank.

Trinity Church was designed by George W. Brimmer and built in 1829 at the corner of Summer and Hawley Street and was so admired that it was called "The Bower of Taste" when it was built. The Gothic Revival church, with its crenelated tower, was somewhat cumbersome and with its rough-hewn granite blocks was described as a "massive temple of rough-hewn granite and ponderous square front tower." The Boston Mercantile Building was on the right of the church at 32 Summer Street and the carpeting establishment of Joseph Lovejoy and Sons was on the left of the church at 14 Summer Street with Thorndike Hall on the far left near Washington Street.

The Church of the Savior was designed by J. H. Hammatt Billings and was built in 1846 on Bedford Street. In 1854, the church united with the Second Church in Boston, and the cojoined congregation worshipped in the Church of the Savior. As many of the parishioners had moved away from the neighborhood, the church was disassembled in 1872 with the stone being stored, and the land was sold. A year later, the church was reassembled with slight modifications by Nathaniel Bradlee on Boylston Street facing Copley Square in Boston's Back Bay where it remained until 1914 when it moved to Audubon Circle.

St. Stephen's Episcopal Church was a free church that was established by Dr. Eleazer Porter Wells. Built in 1845 on Purchase Street, the expense of its land and construction was donated by William Appleton, who also endowed the church. Wells was ordained deacon in the Protestant Episcopal Church by Bishop Brownell in 1827, and he served at the "House of Reformation … [for] six years, until he was requested to found the Farm School on Thompson's Island, Boston, in 1834. In 1835, he established a school of his own at City Point, called 'The School of Moral Discipline.' Here he worked for many years, until his health and strength completely failed him, when he sold out the establishment."

Franklin Street in Boston was originally laid out in the 1790s by noted architect Charles Bulfinch, and included rowhouses on both sides of an elliptical curve. Known as the Tontine Crescent, this was an upscale neighborhood in the first half of the nineteenth century, but by the 1850s, the city was expanding commercially. The row-houses were demolished, but the gentle elliptical arc of Bulfinch's Tontine Crescent was maintained with the rebuilding of new commercial blocks in 1859. Looking towards Federal Street, with Arch Street on the right, the four- and five-story buildings commanded the streetscape and were the pride and joy of the city. In the center distance can be seen the Cathedral Building. These buildings did not last long, as they were destroyed in the Great Boston Fire of 1872.

Franklin Street, looking towards Washington Street, was the epitome of Boston's growth in the mid-nineteenth century and was a proud manifestation of the city's architectural and mercantile achievements. Gridley J. Fox Bryant was an architect who built in granite with what his father Gridley Bryant had quarried in Quincy. In the center of Franklin Street was a 100-foot municipal flagpole that was surmounted by a gilded ball. On the right is the Revere Bank, and a partial view of Francis Skinner & Company. This was the New Boston of the early 1870s and it evoked a sense of pride.

The Cathedral Building was designed by Joseph E. Billings and built on the site of the Cathedral of the Holy Cross, a Roman Catholic church designed by Charles Bulfinch and built in 1803 at Franklin and Devonshire Streets. It was established by Jean Lefebvre de Cheverus, First Catholic Bishop of Boston, and when Pope Pius VII created the Diocese of Boston the church was elevated to a cathedral. The building proved too small for the city's increasing Catholic population and was enlarged in 1825. The last mass was in 1860 and the church was demolished in 1862. Patrick Donahue bought the land and had the impressive Cathedral Building built, where the *Boston Pilot* was printed. It also was the location of the Emigrant Savings Bank and other stores. (*Author's collection*)

The Beebe Block was an impressive five-story commercial block with a Mansard roof that was built at Devonshire and Otis Streets at Winthrop Square. Built in 1861, the block was named for owner James Madison Beebe, a successful dry goods merchant. Beebe was credited with being one of the first men, if not the first, in his line of business to introduce the system of cash payments. His motto was "quick money and small profits," and he was known to sell at a 5 percent advance when other merchants were receiving an advance of 10 or 15 percent. The store carried on an enormous trade in dry goods with all parts of the country, and was especially strong in the great panic of 1857. At that time, Beebe was rated as the largest jobber of dry goods in New England, and second in the country only to Alexander Stewart of New York. He was also the second largest importer in the United States, and at one time transacted a business of $5,000,000 annually. Seen here were also the Parker Wilder & Company and Whitten, Burdett & Young Company, dry goods stores. (*Author's collection*)

The corner of Franklin and Devonshire Street had the National Revere Bank of Boston on the ground floor with the Edward G. Tileston Company, the Charles H. Mills, and the Wm. R. Lovejoy Company on the upper floors. The bank was established as a State Bank in 1859 and eventually was reorganized under the National Banking Laws in 1865. It was said that "The National Revere Bank, by a just and honorable course, has secured a prominent position among the solid financial institutions of the United States, and fully merits the entire confidence of the community."

2

AN EPIZOOTIC IN BOSTON

There was an epizootic in the fall of 1872 that affected the horses of Boston. It was devastating, especially as horses were important in not just pulling carriages and carts, but also the streetcars that crisscrossed the city of Boston. Seen here is Streetcar 86 that connected Boston, via the South End, to Roxbury, terminating at the Norfolk House on Roxbury Meeting House Hill. With most of the horses in Boston suffering from the equine flu in November of 1872, conductors and passengers are depicted in this etching pulling a streetcar along its tracks during the epizootic. Even Edward Savage, chief of police, said on October 26: "The horse disease commenced in Boston, making it necessary to propel fire engines, horse cars, and other vehicles through the streets with human muscle."

THE GREAT EPIZOOTIC OF 1872

In the fall of 1872, Boston was in the throes of an equine influenza that affected horses, most of whom began to show symptoms such as a cough and general sluggishness. The disease was said to have emanated from Canada and within weeks the symptoms had become prevalent in major cities. Horses showed a series of common symptoms, including discharges from the nostrils and eyes, a rasping cough, general exhaustion, and an inability to work. Those symptoms and the images of sick horses were so ubiquitous they became the subject of satire, as in an etching of an ill horse called a *Cheval-Rous Patient*, which appeared in *Harper's Weekly*. However this was a serious situation, as the impact on Boston by the affected horses was devastating, especially as horses were vital in not just pulling carriages and carts, but also the delivery of goods, foods and supplies. The result was that manpower was necessary and it extended to the transportation of fire engines, if needed at a fire. With most of the horses in cities suffering with the equine flu, the *Detroit Free Press* said on October 26, 1872 that horses worsened with a "dry and hacking cough, moving with reluctance and general dullness; nasal membranes at first pale; watery discharge from one or both nostrils; ears and legs cold."

It was greatly feared that the epizootic would affect humans, but the ill horses seriously impacted the economy by cutting off cities from crucial supplies of food and fuel just as winter was approaching. As one newspaper editor said, horses were literally the "wheels in our great social machine, the stoppage of which means widespread injury to all classes and conditions of persons." It was commented that "Boston nearly burned to the ground because fire departments there had lost most of their horses." As the horses in Boston were too ill to be of service, Fire Chief John Damrell had no choice but to bring in groups of men to drag the engines laden down with water hose reels and ladders to the fire. After the fire had been quelled, a city commission investigated the fire and found that fire crews' response times were delayed by pulling the fire engines. The city began to replace horse drawn engines with steam-powered equipment so as to not be dependent on horses in the future.

This etching of a *Cheval-Rous Patient* appeared in *Harper's Weekly* on November 16, 1872 and depicts a horse suffering from the epizootic with his hooves in a warm pail of water, a blanket around his shoulders, and a steaming hot toddy and medicine beside him. Henry Bergh had founded the American Society for the Prevention of Cruelty to Animals in 1866 which was the nation's first organization devoted to the prevention of animal cruelty. In the fall of 1872, he would stop carriages, wagons, and horse-drawn trolleys to inspect the horses for signs of the disease; however, it was to spread throughout the country, severely affecting urban areas. An ill horse was quoted as saying "Ungrateful man never appreciated my faithful services until now. When I am convalescent, I hope he will treat me with more consideration and kindness."

A CHEVAL-ROUS PATIENT.

Nancy Furstinger said that during the epizootic "People were forced to transform into beasts of burden, using pushcarts and wheelbarrows to transport the merchandise that was piling up at docks." The conditions under which horses lived were partially blamed for the outbreak. "The car and stage horses of this city suffer invariably from all possible forms of equine disease ... badly fed, worse housed, overworked, and never groomed, they are ready victims of disease." The 1872 outbreak crippled the economy, impacted all transportation (steamboats, railroads, canals, streetcars), led to permanent changes in Americans' lives, and was said to be one of the major causes of the Panic of 1873. Theodore R. Davis sketched *The Horse Plague* for *Harper's Weekly* on November 16, 1872.

Ruined and Winter at the Door—An Episode of the Horse Plague was a sketch that appeared in *Harper's Weekly* on November 23, 1872. The horse epizootic highlighted the desperation of thousands of Americans who depended on their horses for their livelihood. In the nineteenth century, horses lived and worked in large numbers throughout the United States. According to Ann Norton Greene "Horses powered almost every aspect of urban life." Their populations were concentrated in cities and flourished with the rapid urban growth of the late nineteenth century. The epizootic disease was characterized in this rather superficial poem by "D. M. J." printed in the *Indianapolis Journal*, November 22, 1872:

> *Not a sound was heard in the silent street,*
> *As home from the concert, we hurried;*
> *For we found not a street car, carriage or bus,*
> *And we felt considerably worried.*
> *We hailed a driver we used to know*
> *And hurriedly asked the reason;*
> *He said, as he sadly shook his head,*
> *That the horses were all sneezin.*

Firemen and volunteer members of Torrent Six on Eustis Street in Roxbury stand in front of the firehouse with their Hunneman engine in the doorway. This was a fire company that had firemen, seen on the right with leather helmets, which would pull their engine by hand along Washington Street through the South End to the fire. Notice the mascot laying on the sidewalk, which ironically is not a dalmatian. Edward S. Savage, chief of police in Boston, said on October 26, 1872: "The

horse disease commenced in Boston, making it necessary to propel fire engines, horse cars, and other vehicles through the streets with human muscle."

3

THE LURID LIGHT OF A BURNING CAULDRON

Boston, as the Eagle and the Wild Goose See It was a detail of a photograph taken by James Wallace Black in 1860 from Samuel King's hot-air balloon the "Queen of the Air." In 1863, Oliver Wendell Holmes wrote in the *Atlantic Monthly*: "Boston, as the eagle and wild goose see it, is a very different object from the same place as the solid citizen looks up at its eaves and chimneys. The Old South and Trinity Church are two landmarks not to be mistaken. Washington Street slants across the picture as a narrow cleft. Milk Street winds as if the old cow path which gave it a name had been followed by the builders of its commercial palaces. Windows, chimneys, and skylights attract the eye in the central parts of the view, exquisitely defined, bewildering in numbers." This is the area of Boston from Washington Street east to wharves along the waterfront was destroyed on November 9 and 10, 1872.

The Klous Building where the fire began was at 83 Summer Street was sketched by Sidney L. Smith. It was at the corner of Kingston Street and was owned by Seman Klous, a wealthy merchant and an incorporator of the *Boston Globe*. The ground floor was rented to Tebbetts, Baldwin and Davis Company, wholesale dry goods merchants; the second floor to Damon, Temple & Company, dealers in men's furnishing goods; and the upper floors to Alexander Young Company, which manufactured hoopskirts and bustles and sold corsets. The fire started in the basement of the building around 7:00 p.m. and the alarm was raised at 7:24 p.m. with the call board at city hall indicating that Box 52 had been pulled. By 8:00 p.m., all of Boston's twenty-one engine companies were on the scene. The flames leapt from one Mansard roof to another in the crowded commercial district, and within minutes whole blocks were consumed by fire. (*Author's collection*)

Boston Fire November 8, 1872 (actually November 9) was painted by Fred E. Phelps. This painting shows the fire spreading along the docks seen from East Boston across Boston Harbor. There is a ship in the harbor and small boats, but the fire illuminated the night sky and attracted large numbers of curious people who either gathered to watch the fire or from afar, but Bostonians viewed the blaze as an awesome spectacle. (*Courtesy Coyle's Auction Inc., Nancy Wyman*)

The Lurid Glare of the Flames Lighted Up the Entire City

The fire had begun in the Klous Building on Summer Street which was engulfed in flames within minutes. The fury of the fire rose to the wood-framed Mansard roof that burnt out of the reach of firehoses and continued unabated until the flames inevitably spread from one Mansard roof to the next. The heat from the burning buildings, the geysers of sparks and embers became infernal and its intensity caused the granite facades to implode, falling to the street. It was said that "Blocks of granite, weighing tons, were split as if by powder, and hurled across wide streets." The fire spread and Russell Conwell remembered:

> In a falling building on Franklin Street there were seen through the flashes of fire the forms of men attempting to leap from the windows; but they never reached the pavement: their cries were heard above the crashing timbers and the noise of explosions, awakening shrilly echoes in the ears of those who heard, which will never cease to call. At the time of the fire, the face of the granite was peeled off like a chestnut in a toaster; and great granite-chips tumbled to the ground as if an invisible hand with mallet and steel was at work, bent on defacing the smooth surface and sharp lines with all the haste possible.

Facades of the commercial blocks fell with a sudden roar, sending up showers of sparks and cinders, and as well as a lurid black smoke that enveloped the streets. However, it was not just commercial block that were aflame, even churches were engulfed by fire.

> [Reverend Phillips Brooks was] sitting in one of the pews of Trinity Church, with Mr. Dillon the sexton, resting after the fatigues of the awful night, when the flames were seen stealing in at the roof of the northeast corner. They waited there together, watching the progress of the flames until it became unsafe to remain. As they were hurriedly leaving the building, Mr. Dillon, in his excitement, threw open the great doors of the tower and fastened them back, as had been his habit for many years when the congregation was to disperse after service was over, this last time, as it were, for the invisible crowd of witnesses to take their final departure.

Once the pride of Boston, the imposing commercial buildings were destroyed, block by block. Henry Ward Beecher said poignantly: "Architecture has done its best; and yet the flame has puffed out its lips at them, and they are gone."

John S. Damrell, in a lithograph by E. R. Howe, is seen with his initials on his belt buckle holding his leather helmet with its chief badge and his brass speaking trumpet under his arm. "Damrell was elected to the position of Chief Engineer of Boston Fire Department in 1866. He warned city officials about the danger of fire in the business district. He is concerned with the water supply, shortage of fire hydrants, lack of fire equipment, and the density of tall buildings with wooded mansard roofs in the district. Recognizing the need for long-term improvements in construction practices, he also advocated for the establishment of a building department and building inspection services with the authority to enforce fire and building codes. Boston finally passes an ordinance for 'Regulation and Inspection of Buildings' in June of 1871." (*Collection Boston Athenaeum*)

The American Fireman, Always Ready was depicted in an 1858 print by Currier and Ives of a fireman in his coat and leather helmet pulling a horseless fire engine. The artist Louis Maurer depicted the heroism of the firefighters and volunteers who respond to fires. The aspect of the fireman pulling his engine out of the firehouse was something which occurred in 1872 when the horses of the city's fire department stables were affected by the epizootic. However the water pressure and supply was totally inadequate for the five-story buildings with wood-framed Mansard roofs. (*Author's collection*)

The Outbreak of the Great Boston Fire is an etching done by Sidney Lawton Smith looking east on Summer Street from Washington Street showing the fire having engulfed the building at 83 Summer Street, with people running to the scene. This scene was published in the early twentieth century by Charles E. Goodspeed, a noted book dealer and antiquarian on Beacon Hill.

Loud through the still November air the clang and clash of
fire-bells broke;
From street to street, from square to square, rolled sheets
of flame and clouds of smoke. The marble structures reeled
and fell, the iron pillars bowed like lead;
But one lone spire rang on its bell above the flames.

Hezekiah Butterworth

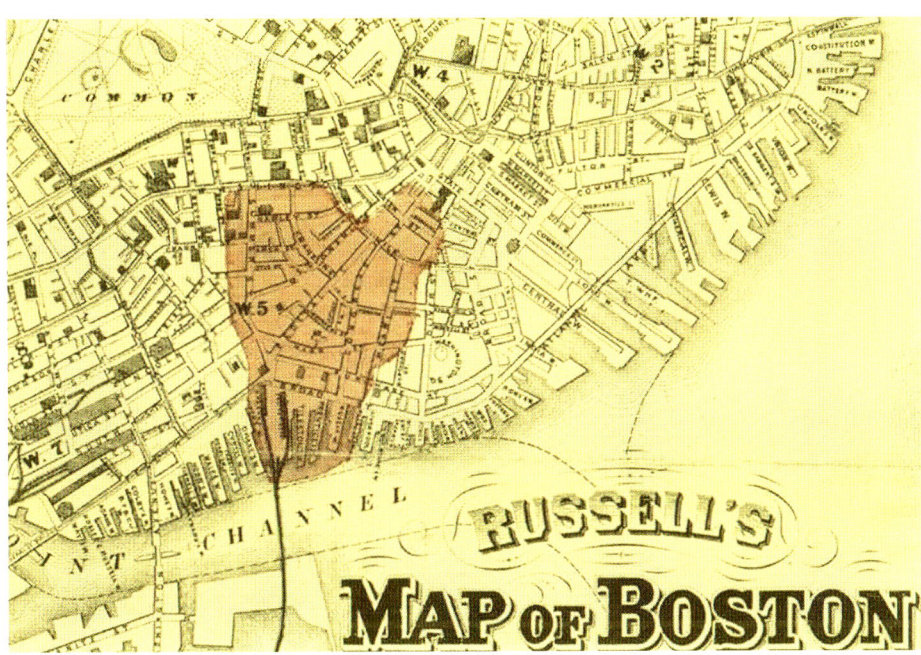

A detail of *Russell's Map of Boston* has the Burnt District highlighted, which shows the 65 acres that were destroyed by the fire. From Washington Street to the waterfront, bound by Summer Street on the left and Milk Street on the right, it was a devastating loss not just to Boston, but would impact the economy. The wharves along Broad Street at the waterfront are, *from left to right*: Piper Wharf with the Boston, Hartford & New Haven Railroad Station and Freight Depot, Tileston Wharf, Prentice Wharf, Russia Wharf, Pearl Street Wharf, and Liverpool Wharf.

This print by B. B. Russell Company showed the triumvirate of Boston in 1872; William Gaston, mayor of Boston in 1872, John S. Damrell, chief of the fire department, and Edward H. Savage, chief of police. The fire would eventually destroy a large fan-shaped swath of the commercial district of the city. Mayor Gaston was roundly criticized by the newspapers for failing to show decisive leadership during attempts to bring the fire under control.

The Boston Fire: A View of Boston from Across the Harbor in East Boston is a painting by F. William Shaw that was painted in 1876. John Damrell, the city's fire engineer, described the fire: "The conflict raged for fifteen hours with an unrelenting fury [and it was the] most terrific engagement by the fire department for superiority over the fire fiend ever recorded in the annals of the city." (*Collection Boston Athenaeum*)

O vision of that sleepless night,
What hue shall paint the mocking light.
That burned and stained the orient skies,
Where peaceful morning loves to rise.

Oliver Wendall Holmes, Sr.

The Boston Daily Globe on November 11, 1872 graphically described the intensity of the fire: "Whole blocks were literally mowed down by the flames like wheat before the reaper's scythe.... Granite was of no more avail against them than so much cardboard." This etching by J. N. Hyde shows the fire ravaging Washington Street, looking south towards Milk Street and the Old South Meeting House. The newspaper said: "The heat now became infernal. The streets ran rivers of water, and every moment was heard the sound of granite blocks exploding and falling in the streets, making them impassable." (*Author's collection*)

Boston—Into the Jaws of Death was sketched by Charles Stanley Reinhart and published in *Harper's Weekly, Journal of Civilization* on November 30, 1872. It depicts firemen fiercely combating the fire, laying hose and valiantly streaming inadequate water supplies on the five story commercial buildings engulfed in flames. As the fire intensified, the streets were increasingly filled with spectators as well as looters and merchants, some looking to pilfer and others trying to save their property. Reverend Rollin Neale of the First Baptist Church of Boston said: "The firemen who labored nobly to stay the flames are entitled to gratitude." (*Author's collection*)

This sketch by J. J. Harley depicts *Washington Street looking south with the Ruins of the Chickering Building and the Globe Theatre on the left.* It was imperative to keep people from the burning buildings as "Blocks of granite weighing tons, were split as if by powder, and hurled across wide streets, and planks went flying through the air as if they were feathers." However, according to Lucius Beebe it was also the fact that "Youths, smelling like the Medford [rum] distillery, whirled and revolved and fell down with screams of laughter in the gutters for all the world as though it were Fourth of July." The scene of the fire was at once frightening but had all the overtures of a carnival with curious people descending upon the spectacle. (*Author's collection*)

The gold moon, 'gainst a copper sky, hung like a portent in the air,
The midnight came, the wind rose high, and men stood speechless in despair.
But, as the marble columns broke, and wider grew the chasm red,
A seething gulf of flame and smoke

Hezekiah Butterworth

Harper's Weekly on November 30, 1872 had an etching showing the desperate fight against the fire which was soon complicated by mobs of frenzied businessmen trying to salvage their wares and ledgers, looters eager to grab what they could, and hordes of curious onlookers. Seen on the left, a dry goods merchant fights off a looter as others go through the goods he has already saved from the fire in the foreground. Since the fire was not threatening residential areas, many Bostonians viewed the blaze as an awesome spectacle. Gawkers, by some counts as many as 10,000, and many of them inebriated, added to the firefighters' struggle.

Flown Away as an Eagle Toward Heaven

The fire burnt throughout the night, creating a macabre scene that could only be likened to that of Dante Alighieri's *Inferno*. Overworked firemen, frantic merchants, and curious onlookers made the scene one of utter chaos. The fire was so intense that men could see "the light flaming against the midnight sky, growing wider, broader and higher. It flames so high that it becomes a beacon-light to mariners three hundred miles away; so bright that it gilds, not only the dome of the State House, and surrounding spires but lights up the Blue Hills of Milton."

The epicenter of the conflagration was engulfed in flames. Frothingham said that "Blocks of granite weighing tons, were split as if by powder, and hurled across wide streets, and planks went flying through the air as if they were feathers." People screaming, firemen yelling orders with no one paying any heed, and "the crash of falling blocks of granite, the hum of engines, the roar of the seething flames, the hiss of steam as immense volumes of water were poured in upon the burning mass, and the shouting of the firemen, made up a Babel of horrible sounds—it was like a pandemonium."

The heat was so intense that firemen sought cover as they played their hoses on the fire. Crowds of frantic onlookers moved from area to area as the fire swept whole streets in less than an hour. As the fire ravaged the buildings, "Iron shutters were warped and melted; granite columns crumbled and fell; while the great piles of cotton and woolen fabrics furnished fuel for the fire, which gleamed with a horrid glare, engulfing everything combustible in the general ruin." *The History of the Great Conflagration* describes the scene:

> The wind had increased to nearly a gale, and the flames having the entire mastery of everything, swept from story to story, from roof to roof, from block to block, and from corner to corner, driving the firemen from every vantage ground they could secure, and rendering all their exertions useless and futile. Whenever the flames reached they rapidly consumed everything of a combustible nature, even melting granite blocks and iron doors and shutters like so much lead.

Rev. V. M. Simons of the Bromfield Methodist-Episcopal Church summarized it:

> Standing amid the wreck of our ruined hopes, with the accumulations of a lifetime of hard industry swept from us, with riches of stocks and stores, merchandise and estates, flown away as an eagle toward heaven, it behooves us to accept the situation in the spirit of serious self-examination, and with reverent attention to the voice of that Providence which admonishes us not to set our eyes upon things so vain, vexatious, and uncertain as earthly possessions.

Louisa May Alcott remarked: "The Common was a scene of constant activity, for the poor shop keepers carried their goods there & stacked them up in great heaps with men to stand guard." In fact, it was "a convenient asylum for all sorts of household goods. Pots, kettles and pans, beds and bedbugs, crying women and hungry babies were plentiful enough" laying on the grass. Seen here in the *Supplement to Frank Leslie's Newspaper*, men unload crates from a tipcart just inside the Park Street Gate, seen on the right, with the caption: "Terrified citizens removing valuables to a place of safety."

This etching *Excitement in State Street—Removal of Papers and Valuables* was sketched for *The Illustrated London News*, December 7, 1872. Seen in front of the post office (the former Merchants' Exchange) on State Street, hundreds of people create a chaotic scene as they try to save things from the various banks, offices, and countinghouses, some using push carts as the fire continued to spread towards the area.

The state militia with rifles and bayonets guarded the entrance to Congress Street. It was said by Russell Conwell that "The militia-men were on guard around and about the burnt quarter for two weeks, day and night. On the Monday morning after the fire they formed a stern, unbroken line from Avon Place, along Washington Street to Water; through Water to Devonshire; along Devonshire, through Congress Square, to Congress Street; through Congress to State; along State to Kilby; through Kilby to Water and Broad; along the Fort-hill territory and the water-front; up along behind Summer Street, Bedford, Kingston, and around again to Avon Place; enclosing a territory of more than a hundred acres."

The Supplement to Frank Leslie's Illustrated Newspaper showed an etching by J. B. Henderson of the "arrival of the special train from Worcester, conveying the Worcester Fire Department, with steam fire engines, to the scene of disaster." The frantic and highly charged scene as a fire engine is removed from the flatbed of the train can be sensed as it was eased onto a ramp and then pulled by hand to the fire as hundreds watch from the sidelines.

General View of the Ruins, From the West Side of Washington Street—The Old South Church and the 'Transcript' Building in the Foreground appeared in *Harper's Weekly* on November 30, 1872. The Old South Church was saved by forty firemen who arrived at North Station from Portsmouth, New Hampshire, with the *Kearsarge 3* pumper engine, the 6,000-pound coal-fired engine. This engine, made by the Amoskeag Manufacturing Company, was to play water on the wood-spire and wood-shingle roof of the church, thereby saving it from the fire. The engine was named for the USS *Kearsarge*, a ship that gained fame in battle during the recent Civil War. The sloop of war, in turn, had been named for a New Hampshire Mountain.

"The Old South must be levelled soon to check the flames and save the street;
Bring fuse and powder." But at noon the ancient fane still stood complete.
The mitred flame had lipped the spire, the smoke its blackness o'er it cast;
Then, hero-like, men fought the fire, and from each lip the watchword passed,—
The Old South stands!

Hezekiah Butterworth

The Great Fire at Boston November 9th & 10th 1872 was a lithograph published by Haskell and Allen, which was located at 61 Hanover Street in Boston. The lithograph shows the city and the waterfront engulfed in flames with billowing clouds of smoke and intense flames of fire. It was said that the fire was so intense that the glow of the flames was noted by ships off the coast of Maine. (*Collection of the Boston Athenaeum*)

4

THE BURNT DISTRICT

The dramatic painting *The Great Fire of 1872* depicts a city ensconced in the infernal glow of the fire with a billowing cloud of smoke. Edward Stanwood recalled "the night sky was grandly illuminated, and a wild shower of burning brands and cinders was passing over the district which was shortly to be devastated." The dome of the Massachusetts State House and the spires of many churches dominate the skyline of the city on the right as the downtown area of Boston is engulfed in flames. Huge clouds of smoke from the burning buildings waft to the heavens as seen from the East Boston waterfront. (*Collection Massachusetts Historical Society*)

> *Beyond the harbor, calm and fair, the sun came up through bars of gold,*
> *Then faded in a wannish glare, as flame and smoke still upward rolled.*
> *The princely structures, crowned with art, where Commerce laid her treasures bare;*
> *the haunts of trade, the common mart, all vanished in the withering air.*

> Hezekiah Butterworth

Looking up Summer Street towards Washington Street, the C. F. Hovey Store can be seen on the left and adjacent to it R. H. Stearns & Co. In the distance are the ruins of Shreve, Crump, and Low that was not destroyed by the fire, but by a gas explosion the following day. Ironically Mr. Crump had saved his precious stock by "emptying the safe which contained the most valuable property of the firm, pearls and diamonds and other precious stones, into two hand bags, and consigned them to [Rev. Phillips] Brooks with directions to carry them to a house on Newbury Street ... taking no certificate of deposit, and offering no bodyguard for protection on the dangerous errand, for the distance was to be walked, and no conveyances were to be had. Under these circumstances, about the hour of two o'clock in the morning, Mr. Brooks executed the commission entrusted to him." (*Collection of Boston Athenaeum*)

The ruins of Trinity Church were almost picturesque with the crenelated tower holding forth on Summer Street, with its windows and doors blown open to allow glimpses into the once sacred space. A group of men stand amongst the debris that covers the sidewalk and street. On the left is a corner of the building with Robbins, Appleton, and Co., owned by Royal E. Robbins and Daniel E. Appleton, and on the right the ruins of the Mercantile Building. Reverend John Beckley of the Somerset Street Baptist Church said: "Dear old Trinity Church! Many tender memories cluster around its smoldering ruins, and its lonely tower brings mingled scenes of joy and sorrow to many minds; but the vital organization, the live church which the granite only symbolized, remains to continue elsewhere the Christian work which for so long a period has centered within the massive walls that crumbled before the flames."

Reverend Phillips Brooks had been Rector of Trinity Church since 1869. He said: "The desolation of the fire is bewildering. Old Trinity seemed safe all night, but toward morning the fire swept into her and there was no chance. She went at four in the morning. I saw her well afire, inside and out, carried off some books and robes, and left her. She went majestically and her great tower stands now, as solid as ever, a most picturesque and stately ruin. She died in dignity. I did not know how much I liked the gloomy old thing until I saw her windows bursting and the flame running along her high old pews." (*Author's collection*)

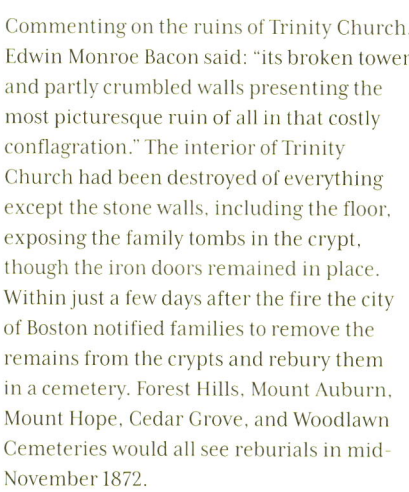

Commenting on the ruins of Trinity Church, Edwin Monroe Bacon said: "its broken tower and partly crumbled walls presenting the most picturesque ruin of all in that costly conflagration." The interior of Trinity Church had been destroyed of everything except the stone walls, including the floor, exposing the family tombs in the crypt, though the iron doors remained in place. Within just a few days after the fire the city of Boston notified families to remove the remains from the crypts and rebury them in a cemetery. Forest Hills, Mount Auburn, Mount Hope, Cedar Grove, and Woodlawn Cemeteries would all see reburials in mid-November 1872.

The Claflin Guards, Newton Company C, 1st Regiment Massachusetts Militia, are drawn up in formation on Kilby Street. Mayor William Gaston had requested "as Sunday drew to a smoky and hysterical close that, exhausted as they were, the ... [police] would not be sufficient to maintain order throughout the city ... six battalions of the state militia were mobilized and, although martial law was never declared so that these had no actual authority, the crowds naturally imagined they had and their presence was respected accordingly." Seen in the center is Captain William Barnas Sears, on the left 1st Lieutenant F. Barnes, and on the right 2nd Lieutenant W. Stearns in front of the militia drawn up in formation. The Claflin Guards was named for Governor William Claflin, who served as governor from 1869 to 1872. The guard was attached at first to the First Regiment of Infantry, making that an eleven-company organization and it was known as L Company of that regiment.

Boston Policemen pose for a group photograph in the Burnt District, looking towards Franklin Street. At the time of the fire there were roughly 500 policemen under the direction of Chief Edward H. Savage in the city with a population of just over 250,000 people. *Continued on next page*

Continued from previous page: On the right is the partially built post office and sub-treasury with its unfinished roof. The building was to block the fire's progress northward, and though damaged by the intensity of the heat, it survived and was completed in 1878.

The area of Milk and Federal Streets were the ruins of Wright and Potter, the state printer; the company was owned by Albert J. Wright and Robert K. Potter. Though the building was destroyed, the tall brick chimney marks the spot of the business, which has a sign stating that they have relocated to 34 School Street. Members of the Claflin Guard are seen on the right with rifles protecting the Burnt District. Boston had become "a vast city of ruins, the limit of which could at no point be seen, still smoking and steaming violently from the shock that had caused its fearful overthrow."

Colonel Russell Conwell in his book *History of the Great Fire in Boston* describes the Burnt District: "In the stead of noble buildings of granite and marble and brick were huge, giant walls, torn and ragged, and broken columns of stone and iron. The lines of the streets were entirely obliterated; and the ways were so blocked by great bowlders of granite, and heaps of debris,—in some places from three to ten feet deep,—that those who had been most familiar with the section before the fire were utterly unable to find their way, and groped about, or clambered over the obstructing rock, brick, iron, and still hot rubbish, dazed and bewildered." These men pose on the ruins for the photographer.

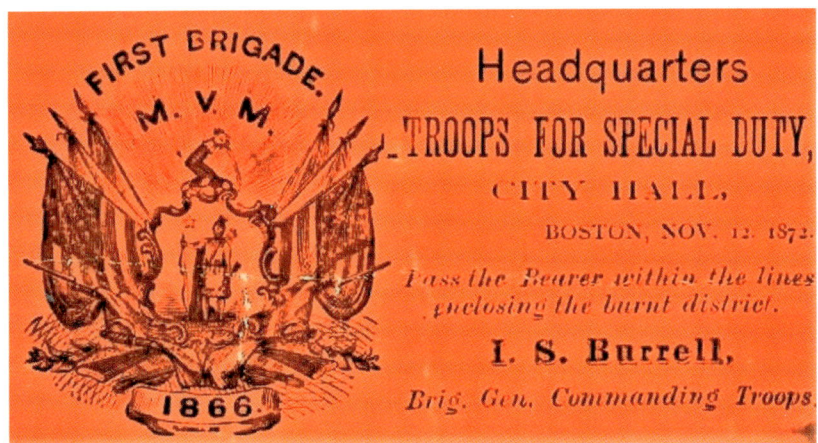

The *Boston Sunday Herald* said on November 10, 1872: "The Most Costly and Valuable Warehouses and Mercantile Establishments Laid in Ashes!" This printed pass was issued by I. S. Burrell, brigadier general commanding troops of the First Brigade Massachusetts Volunteer Militia, to curtail curious people from entering the Burnt District and to prevent them from scavenging, creating havoc or injuring themselves in the ruins of the fire. This pass permitted a person to pass the lines encircling the Burnt District, but only under certain conditions. (*Collection of Boston Athenaeum*)

Members of the Sheridan's Rifle Guard, soldiers under Major General Philip Sheridan of Civil War fame, were quartered at the Old South Meeting House, which was still an active place of worship at the time of the fire. A new church was to be built in Copley Square in 1876. Here soldiers pose for a photograph, some leaning on the high box pews, others standing on them, as they were on break from their guard duty. For weeks following the fire, the Burnt District was encircled by a double line of soldiers with bayonets. The box pews, which once served as seats for worshippers, now served as hard beds for the soldiers.

The Ruins of Boston was painted by John J. Enneking and is a striking scene in its graphic realism of the devastating fire. It was almost as if "A thick, blood-red cloud [was] hovering over the city," as the *Boston Globe* article from November 11, 1872 said, "filling the hearts of all with an ominous and indefinable mixture of terror and sadness." Lucius Beebe said: "Sunday morning dawned on a tremendous yellow pillar of smoke which rolled, like a symbol of doom, slowly over the harbor." On the left is the spire of the Park Street Church with the dome of the State House. (*Collection Massachusetts Historical Society, on loan to the Parkman House*)

> *As if the sun had lost his way*
> *And dawned to make a second day,—*
> *Above how red with fiery glow,*
> *How dark to those it woke below!*

Oliver Wendell Holmes, Sr.

John J. Enneking (1841–1916,) seen in a portrait by Isaac H. Caliga from 1884, was an American Impressionist painter associated with the Boston School of Art. Enneking painted many scenes and his favorite subject was said to be the November twilight of New England, and more generally the half lights of early spring, late autumn, and winter dawn and evening. This portrait is in keeping with Enneking's painting style as Caliga had studied under Wilhelm Lindenschmidt in Munich, German in 1879, remaining there until 1883. The artist was of German descent and his surname Caliga was the Latin translation of his given surname of Stiefel. He became well known in Boston and exhibited this portrait at the Boston Art Club, where he exhibited from 1885 to 1909 and was awarded numerous medals.

Shreve, Crump, and Low was located at the corner of Summer and Washington Street. Founded in 1796 by watchmaker and silversmith John McFarlane, it is one of the oldest jewelry stores in America. The store was not destroyed by the fire but by a gas explosion in the adjacent building of William R. Storms & Co. with the flames destroying the store of Shreve, Crump & Low and the upper floors Wheeler & Wilson, sewing machine warerooms, and Lott & Brett, engravers. The gas was still running through the lines and served as fuel to the fire, with many of Boston's gas lines having exploded due to the fire until the gas could be turned off.

Washington Street, between Milk and Summer Streets, saw utter devastation with most of the buildings leveled. The white marble facade in the center was that of Macullar, Williams and Parker, Clothing and Gentlemen's Furnishing Goods at 200 Washington Street. The business was owned by Addison Macullar, G. B. Williams, C. W. Parker, N. D. Robinson, I. B. Fenton, J. L. Wesson, and H. Foster and produced readymade suits, a novelty at the time. The facade not only survived the fire but was reincorporated into the facade of the new building that was built on the site.

THE BURNT DISTRICT

John Damrell, the city's fire engineer, was an integral witness to the destruction of the area by fire, and described its progress: "The conflict raged for fifteen hours with an unrelenting fury" and was the "most terrific engagement by the fire department for superiority over the fire fiend ever recorded in the annals of the city." One can only imagine the confusion and anxiety of the firemen as fire chiefs shouted orders from their fire trumpets to men who could hardly hear above the roar of the fire and shouting spectators. Even if they could hear, the scene was one of such utter chaos that it only increased with time. A lack of water power from inadequate sources and the fact that water could only reach to the third story of the five-story buildings daunted the efforts of the firemen who watched and were unable to do anything to check the fire's spread. In addition, people were hindering the efforts of the firefighters and something had to be done.

Russell Conwell said:

> Cordons of soldiery with fixed bayonets kept off the pressing crowd, or, capturing a host of citizens between two lines reaching from curb to curb, marched them to side-streets, and gently expelled them from the vicinity of the crumbling and overhanging ruins. The roll of the drum was heard on every side; the sonorous "Fall in" echoed; and those turbulently inclined among such of the spectators as had not directly felt the sting of loss by the conflagration were speedily subdued by the militia-men, who seemed to bear a full sense of their importance.

If one was standing in the midst of the ruins, and looking about him, seeing noting the sentinels bearing guns with bayonets, the towering walls rent and torn in every direction, the broken pillars and iron-work, the huge heaps of jagged granite-blocks and debris under his feet, could easily imagine himself gazing upon a great city destroyed but a brief time before by a terrific bombardment.

The fire had destroyed much of the city east of Washington Street but the wharves projecting into Boston Harbor were also affected and the fire smoldered and burnt, which created havoc for days. Charles Hatch said of the fire: "I can hardly realize that the best part of the business center of Boston is a pile of smoldering ruins." In *Harper's Weekly* on December 7, 1872, the newspaper showed sketches of the coal mounds along the wharves. The article stated:

> On the great docks which formed one boundary of the burned district of Boston were stored many thousands of coal, which took fire, and continued burning with a steady intensity for days after the progress of the flames among the stores and warehouses had been checked, notwithstanding

the streams of water constantly poured upon them. The burning heaps had the appearance of small volcanoes, especially at night, when the dull red glare of the smoldering coal was reflected on the vapor and smoke that hung over them.

Louisa May Alcott said: "All day Sunday the fire burned & last night the sky still glowed red with the tons of coal smoldering on the wharves & small fires breaking out all over the burnt district. Soldiers guarded the streets, for tottering walls were dangerous & thieves so thick the police had no place to hold them when caught." It was said:

> The scenes within the lines of the ruins were novel and picturesque in the extreme. They were bits of pictures only, considering the magnitude of the devastated territory. For three days the smoke was so thick and blinding, that no extended view could anywhere be had. There were life and energy and spirit at every hand. Here, in the midst of huge heaps of hot bricks, surrounded by fires yet smoldering and crackling, men were pushing the work of clearing away the wrecks, which had begun at the very break of dawn on Monday, or of digging out the buried safes and vaults, and crowded about them, picturesquely grouped, were many interested spectators.

Within two days, the fire consumed an area of 65 acres of Boston that included 775 buildings, costly merchandise, and a sense of security. The Burnt District as it was called was encircled by the militia for weeks after the fire, preventing the curious from entering the area either to view the ruins or to wreak havoc.

> *The cloud still hovers overhead,*
> *And still the midnight sky is red;*
> *As the lost wanderer strays alone*
> *To seek the place he called his own,*
> *His devious footprints sadly tell*
> *How changed the pathways known so well;*
> *The scene, how new! The tale, how old*
> *Ere yet the ashes have grown cold!*

Oliver Wendell Holmes

Washington Street, looking towards the Old South Meeting House at the corner of Milk Street, had huge pieces of granite strewn along the street that had simply imploded and crashed to the ground during the fire. On the right is the ruins of the C. Fowle and Son Carpet Company and a row of three-story commercial buildings, of which the *Boston Transcript* was at the far end. The left side of Washington Street was to remain unscathed by the fire and creates an incongruous scene with its parade of advertising signs.

Washington Street, looking towards Milk Street with the Old South Meeting House, saw devastation on the east side with facades gone and only partial walls surviving the devastating fire. On the far left, there was no damage to the buildings on the west side of Washington Street. In fact, an advertisement of George R. Brine & Company, seen on the left, stated: "The best view in Boston, of the Ruins, from our building." The Old South Meeting House had been saved from the fire and marks the north border to the fire's extent. In the center distance can be seen the roof of the uncompleted post office and sub-treasury.

In the days following the fire, canvas tents and temporary wood sheds with corrugated metal roofs were erected on cleared areas for those working in the Burnt District to rest or have refreshments. Here, in the shadow of the spire of the Old South Meeting House on Milk Street, men are gathered around a liberty pole as they began the arduous job of rolling miles of canvas fire hoses and clearing away the debris which was dumped into Boston Harbor and along what became Atlantic Avenue.

The picturesque quality of the ruins had merchants, clerks, firemen, and men clearing the debris stopping to sit on a granite boulder on the former site of Smith Stebbins Company for their photograph. Russell Conwell said: "Photographers also passed the lines, and perched themselves on stone-heaps in the most picturesque quarters, taking views, and making of themselves pictures which sauntering artists outlined in their notebooks; and many of the class of mysterious vandals who go about o' nights, and are seldom seen disfiguring the landscape of the country, overcame the barriers, and painted and posted on the dead walls, the sides of granite columns, and the flat surface of upturned stone-blocks, advertisements of all manner of notions and nostrums."

The unfinished post office and sub-treasury was described as "a composition of pilasters and columns, and round-arched ornamental windows, proportioned to set off the massive pile of masonry covering an area of nearly 45,000 feet of land." Though a portion of the roof and much of the interior was destroyed, the building survived the fire and was completed in 1878 and was to become one of the city's most monumental nineteenth-century buildings which commanded Post Office Square.

The post office and sub-treasury is seen from the ruins of Freeland, Harding and Richardson Company on Devonshire Street and though the area in the foreground had been destroyed by the fire, the nearly completed building stopped the fire. In the *History of the Great Conflagration*, it stated that "the roof was entirely burned off, and also the inside cleaned out; but its immense valuable contents were safely removed to the Custom House." Workers and curious onlookers are on either side of a huge mound of debris that they remove one shovelful at a time.

Reverend Phillips Brooks of Trinity Church recounted on November 12, 1872: "Last Saturday night and Sunday were fearful. For a time, it seemed as if the thing would never stop so long as there was anything left to burn. Everybody has suffered, almost everybody severely. Very many have lost all. Scores of my parishioners [businesses] have been burned out. But the courage and cheerfulness of everybody is noble and delightful." The rubble in the foreground must have proved daunting, but resilient Bostonians rose to the challenge.

The *Cataract* Engine Company 10, which was housed at the corner of Mount Vernon and River Streets on the flat of Beacon Hill, was used by the fireman on the right to hose down smoke and dust. The engine was an Amoskeag First Size steam pumper, Serial # 337, and was stationed on Congress Street and is seen belching its smoke where it would remain as needed for a few weeks after the fire.

The sun came up through bars of gold,
Then faded in a wannish glare,
As flame and smoke still upward rolled.

Hezekiah Butterworth

Franklin Street had been cleared of debris within a week of the fire and canvas tents and wood sheds had been erected for the numerous workers, including a firemen's encampment, who began clearing the area, but the area was a popular draw and "Photographers also passed the lines, and perched themselves on stone-heaps in the most picturesque quarters, taking views, and making of themselves pictures which sauntering artists outlined in their notebooks." The Burnt District seemed to draw people to it, whether by curiosity, news or plunder but the resilience of Bostonians saw rebuilding efforts begin in early 1873.

A large group of men are seen on Milk Street standing in Liberty Square amongst the ruins of the Burnt District. Were they sharing what news they had gleaned or were they united in grief as to the loss of so many businesses? The buildings in the center were destroyed, but were on the edge of the devastation. In the distance, seen on the right, Milk Street near Atlantic Avenue remained unaffected by the fire.

The ruins of St. Stephen's Episcopal Church stand amongst the rubble on what was once Purchase Street. Reverend Wells recounted: "Hardly was a shred saved from church or house for a memento. Much might have been and ought to have been saved; and I would have done it, had I been permitted. I had not believed that the fire would be allowed to cross to our side of the street. As soon, however, as I saw it was likely to do so I started to begin the removal." The church might have been destroyed, but St. Stephen's House was moved to 14 Oxford Street, "where its works of mercy to the poor and the wicked have been continued to this present. Hundreds of men out of employment flocked into the city, expecting to find abundance of work where there was such a scene of destruction; but the severity of the winter soon set in and checked the work, and hundreds of sufferers were dependent for existence on public relief."

Liberty Square was somewhat cleared of debris withing a week of the fire and a small wood shed with a corrugated metal roof had been built for those helping with the cleanup, which must have seemed like a daunting task. The spire of the Old South Meeting House marks the edge of the north boundary of the fire, with buildings reduced to rubble and many thousands of bricks laying in large heaps. A group of men, with canvas firehoses coiled in the foreground, stand in front of a liberty pole that has been erected in the middle of the square which flies the American flag high over the Burnt District.

5

A Sublime and Awful Sight

Seen from the roof of C. F. Hovey Company on Summer Street, this photograph looks across to what had once been Franklin Street and Milk Street after the Great Fire of 1872. Photographed by A. C. Partridge, one of the many photographers who descended upon the Burnt District to record the devastation in stereoviews. Russell Conwell said: "The vista from the vicinity of Summer Street was grandiose and disheartening. Flames flickered up from time to time from the mass of broken, seared, disjointed masonry, played around the cracked and dismantled bases of the great carved iron pillars, and sometimes burst out vehemently from the interstices of the debris; and great columns of smoke rose majestically into the clear air, and then formed into party-colored clouds which cast dull shadows over the scene. At a little distance in the ruin-field, the smoke almost shut off the view; and the fragmentary wall of an ordinary business-block, or the tottering section of some huge furnace, lately a row of houses, took on fantastic forms." (*Courtesy of Panopticon Imaging, Paul Sneyd*)

Milk Street, which extends from Washington Street to Atlantic Avenue, lay in ruins from the rear of the Old South Meeting House to Oliver Street at Liberty Square. Soldiers stand among granite blocks of the ruins of a building, with many men gathered in the street on the right. "Every bit of vantage-ground, from the dread corner near which the fatal fire began to the water-side and along State, was crowded with the motley groups of spectators, each asking a hundred questions in as many breaths."

Two merchants, one in a bowler and the other in a top hat, a policeman and a man sitting on a board are photographed amongst debris and the ruins of buildings on Arch Street. The tower of Trinity Church is seen in the distance and is enveloped in a haze, creating an almost ethereal scene to the Burnt District. It was said: "Approaching the burned district ... one might readily have fancied himself in a recently captured and bombarded town. The crowds, although gayly dressed and rampant with curiosity, were far from jolly, and looked with frightened and dazzled air on the labyrinth of smoking ruins which had once been a mass of busy avenues of commerce. Boston's center seemed suddenly to have vanished: the 'old familiar paths' existed no longer."

Within a few days of the fire, people were viewing the ruins of the Burnt District with unabashed curiosity. Here two women with their escort stand in front of what was Burr, Taft & Company on Devonshire Street. A reporter for the *New York Tribune* said: "When Chicago was burned the railroads carried thousands of people out of the city ... but at Boston nobody goes away and everybody tries to come in. Even ladies venture into the midst of the furnace. They have been clambering all day over the ruins of their husbands' and fathers' warehouses and listening with a sort of pride to their escorts describing the magnitude of their losses."

Curiosity was one thing, but it was something more like a morbid fascination that drew people from near and far to see the devastation of the Burnt District, with or without a pass. A young girl and her companion, standing at the corner of Kilby and Water Streets, are surrounded by men who pose for their photograph while on their perambulation through the cleared streets. Notice the signs on the right, alerting people as to where businesses have moved in the city.

These two guards flank a young man who stands on a pile of debris that was to be seen throughout the Burnt District. This scene was at the corner of Milk and Federal Streets. The militia was on guard around and about the Burnt District for two weeks, day and night, and created a cordon that encircled almost 100 acres of downtown Boston.

Archway of Ruins depicted what was once the Boston Button Company at 67 Milk Street, and was photographed by J. W. Black as well as sketched for Frank Leslie's *Illustrated Newspaper* on December 14, 1872. It was said: "The archway of ruins on Milk Street is an artistic feat of the fire-fiend, and presents the appearance of some classical ruin of ancient Rome or Greece, Babylon, Thebes or Tyre. The arch is formed by a mass of debris falling over and across two pillars. The spectacle has been the subject of a pretty general examination, the museums and art galleries for the once fading in importance before the curious eye of visitors."

Men sit on granite blocks adjacent to the ruins of 60 Pearl Street, a commercial block that incredibly retains the names of the businesses that were once located here still visible on a stone pier on the right. Among the businesses destroyed in the fire were A. A. Gilmore & Company, J. D. Pike & Company, J. D. Warren & Company, L. T. Jefts & Company, W. D. Farren & Company, and C. E. & S. C. Hayes & Company. (*Collection of Boston Athenaeum*)

A large group of men pose amongst the ruins of the H. M. Williams & Company, a wool brokerage at 42 India Street. Three signs are visible projecting from the rubble, one reading "H.M. Williams & Co., [removed to] 42 India St." Merchants began to put up signs on their lots, telling where they could be found. Among them were a number which were somewhat laughable. One firm stated very curtly, "We have removed from this place" another said, "Closed during the heated term" another, "Gone up, can be seen at No.—" still another, "Gone to Tophet to get cooled off" and still another, "These damaged goods to be sold low, and the building thrown in."

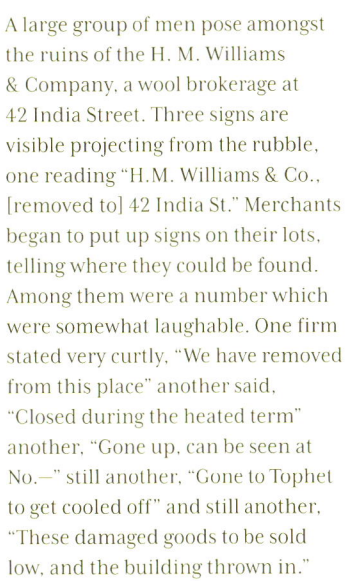

A guard stands in front of the tri-arched entrance to what was once Macullar, Williams and Parker Company on Washington Street, with a sign stating the company removed to 15 Tremont Street. A well-known wholesale and retail dealer of readymade and custom clothing and men's furnishing goods, the store was one of the largest in the city extending from Washington Street to Hawley Street. The facade was of white marble and remarkably survived the fire though the five-story business was completely destroyed. The company stated that all "work-girls, whether heretofore employed by them or not, who might be in need, and they would provide for them; and they further advertised that their pay-roll would be made up on Monday as usual, and requested their employees to come and take their pay."

The H. & J. Pfaff Brewery Company was founded in 1857 by German immigrants Henry and Jacob Pfaff and its beer was made from the good, crisp-tasting water of the Stony Brook in Roxbury to produce not just beer, but the lighter lager. With a large German population in Boston in the 1870s, the Pfaff Brewery was extremely popular. These men, possibly the Pfaff Brothers among them, sit on granite blocks at the site of the former office at 16 Arch Street near Milk Street.

The Ruins were Picturesque and Fascinating

The devastation of the Burnt District was incomprehensible. Streets were covered in granite blocks and mounds of bricks from which iron pillars that had once supported the five-story commercial blocks lay bent and twisted. The area east of Washington Street was one large debris field that attracted the attention of Bostonians. It was said that on that Monday, November 11, 1872:

> … there were pictures of awful desolation and ruin in one great section; and immediately about and around, in marked contrast, pictures of a holiday or gala-day kind…. Where strangers thronged unceasingly from morning till night, looking contented, interested, and happy, watching the calvary as they cantered by, examining the wares of the itinerant peddlers on the Tremont mall, studying the smoky sky through the big telescope, or trying the lung-testers; carrying themselves, for all the world, as if it were a festival they had journeyed hither to see, rather than the destruction of a great section of a great city by fire.

The Burnt District became a lurid attraction, and would remain so for many weeks afterwards:

> Smoke and steam continued to come up in dense volumes out of the cellars; burning leather, and great heaps of coal, yet crackled and roared furiously; and the ruins of vast proportions were yet picturesque and fascinating, and so they remained for some time. The guards during these days were exceedingly strict, acting under orders from headquarters, issued at the request of the city authorities; but many idlers got somehow by them, and constantly perambulated the quarter, loading their pockets and persons with rubbish which they collected as "relics," joining interestedly the groups about the workmen engaged in opening the safes as they were recovered from the ruins in the heaped-up basements, and joining in the expressions of sympathy when it was found—which, alas! was too often the case—that the great iron boxes contained, instead of money and wealth, only ashes and poverty.

Everyone seemed to want a souvenir of the fire to remember the worst catastrophe ever to befall Boston. From objects melded together by the intense heat of the fire to metal plates, cups, bowls and cutlery, all weirdly twisted and that had melted from the fire, everyone sought a memento. For those unable to venture into the Burnt District to search for a relic of their own choosing, there were dozens of men selling curiosities that one could purchase.

It seemed that photographers' stereoviews of the aftermath of the fire were among the most popular, as people often had a handheld stereoscope that allowed them to views a pair of separate images, depicting left-eye and right-eye views of the same scene, as a single three-dimensional image. Numerous professional photographers in Boston including James Wallace Black, John Adams Whipple, John Payson Soule, A. Cheney Partridge, E. E. Smith, H. Ropes & Company, Joseph L. Bates, J. Ward & Son and Benjamin W. Kilburn took photographs of the ruins, projecting walls, debris fields and street scenes, often with people who were fortunate enough to secure a pass to enter the Burnt District, that were avidly collected by curious Bostonians. These graphicly depicted stereo views, even 150 years later, still attest to the devastation and widespread desolation caused by the fire.

In the days and weeks after the fire, the Sheridan Riles Guards, and cadets from the Charlestown Navy Yard became a familiar site in Boston. They were not only guarding the Burnt District:

> [The] Men in blue were moving about, musket in hand, or sleeping in the wide, old-fashioned pews [of the Old South Meeting House.] A group were lounging about the old pulpit, chatting and chaffing; and other knots, engaged apparently in the same comfortable and harmless occupation, were gathered here and there. The light was dim and dismal, coming from tallow-candles stuck into the gas-brackets, and held up from bayonet-points; and the air was sharp and chilling, the shattered windows admitting every breeze.

They remained as a necessary protection, not just of safes but for the safety of people who ventured into the debris fields.

Russell Conwell said: "A week after the terrible devastation, there were little puffs of smoke still visible; but the great piles of broken granite and the shattered walls were silent and grand, reminding one of Pompeii and the crumbling temples of Baalbec and Petræa." The *Cataract* Steamer No. 10 from the Mount Vernon Street firehouse on the Flat of Beacon Hill would remain for weeks in the area of Liberty Square as a backup to quell the smoking ruins. It was still a smoky area as the Burnt District "was a vast city of ruins, the limit of which could at no point be seen, still smoking and streaming violently from the shock that had caused its fearful overthrow."

The business signs of the Palmer & Bachelders Company, silversmiths, and D. C. Percival Jr. & Company, manufacturing jewelers, at 168 Washington Street survived the fire but only the facade of the businesses remains. Soldiers with their rifles over their shoulders guard the entrance before the safes could be extricated from the basement after they fell as the floors burned.

The area of Pearl and Milk Streets is seen looking towards Oliver Street. The area was one of utter desolation, and often impossible to find one's bearings of the former streets. Russell Conwell recounted "in the ruin-field, the smoke almost shut off the view; and the fragmentary wall of an ordinary business-block, or the tottering section of some huge furnace, lately a row of houses, took on fantastic forms." Four militia guards are seen standing on either side a safe that projects from the rubble of the fire.

Franklin Street was devastated with few walls of the once proud granite buildings surviving. This area was, before the fire, "the busiest and wealthiest quarter of the city, and filled with commanding granite, marble, iron, brown-stone and brick buildings. The stock of goods on hand was very large, and almost all became a total loss."

"All things must come to an end, and after eighteen hours of trial Boston emerged from her baptism of fire. In that space of time, it had destroyed hundreds of the costliest and most substantial warehouses in the country." This photograph shows the utter devastation wrought by the fire. Shells of buildings and walls pointing like fingers toward the heavens served as grim reminders of the once urban streetscapes of Boston. The granite blocks in the foreground would be used as infill for Atlantic Avenue.

Though the business once located on this site is unknown, portions of walls survived the fire as did the many cast iron columns which had once supported the upper stories. The cast-iron columns act almost as silent sentinels projecting from the brick and iron-strewn rubble.

The business signs of Davis, Roundy & Cole and the John Earle & Company, tailors, S. Hunt, tailor, proclaim their former inhabitants' businesses at 25 Summer Street, but the fire destroyed everything but the facade. Notice the wood signs on either side of the opening giving information where the businesses moved to.

The ruins of the Ward's Ink Company on Franklin Street looked as if the granite had melted rather than imploded. Samuel Ward had a highly profitable business that offered Ward's Umbrella Cone Ink Bottles, Ward's Gum Stickum, Ward's Diamond Streel pens and Bird's Ink; he also offered a wide assortment of stationary. On the site of what had once been the entrance to the building remains the signs for the occupants. Among them A. A. Gilmore Company, J. D. Pike and others.

Looking east from Washington Street, with the Old South Meeting House on the left, Milk Street was devastated by the fire. A man stands among the rubble of Currier and Trott Company, on the right, that was adjacent to the Boston *Transcript* newspaper. Currier and Trott was owned in 1872 by Richard Currier and Jesse Smith who were silversmiths, jewelers and where they offered foreign and American watches and clocks in their shop.

A merchant stands in front of
Clark Plympton & Company, the
remains of his ruined business at
12 Summer Street. The company
were importers, jobbers & retailers
of china, crockery & glass and
also offered fine plated ware and
cutlery.

Baeder, Adamson & Company
was at 143 Milk Street and were
manufacturers of glue and curled
hair, cow hide whips, sand & emery
paper, neat's-foot, oil, bone, dust,
plastering hair. Founded in 1828, it
became the premier manufacturer
of its kind in the United States.
Charles Baeder and William
Adamson had a successful business
with locations not just in Boston
but also Philadelphia and Chicago;
they also owned the Woburn Glue
and Gelatin Works. The windows
are intact in some places but in the
foreground the south side of Milk
Street was leveled.

A sign, flanked by well-dressed men, says that the building that was once on this site and now in ruins has removed to 65 Chauncy Street.

A horse-drawn wagon is seen near Congress Street. Lucius Beebe said: "By the end of the week the devastated section of the city showed signs of recovered order, and although smoke still curled from numerous cellars and the protective agents were still engaged in tearing down tottering towers and chimneys, little shops, barber's saloons, bars and chop houses were springing into being under canvas [tents] or in hastily erected sheds and pine-board shelters."

A milk wagon from the Consumers Protection Association on Hanover Street in the North End delivered milk and dairy products to those who were working in the Burnt District. There were hundreds of people working in the area, some living in wood shelters, and members of the militia quartered at the Old South Meeting House. This photograph is interesting as it shows the delivery wagon driver holding the reins with a policeman to the right, and men standing on the debris with Milk Street in the distance.

The ruins on Franklin Street of Patrick Donahue's Cathedral Building and the Emigrant Savings Bank, of which he was president, and other shops were a pile of granite blocks that were the remnants of a building that "was frequently compared in grandeur with the Beebe Block." The Cathedral Building had not been insured and Donahue lost $300,000. Undaunted he regrouped and continued to publish *The Pilot*, a weekly paper devoted to Irish-American and Catholic interests, in addition to starting *Donahue's Monthly Magazine* which was described as "a journal devoted to the Irish, at home and abroad."

The B. S. Smith Company, a cotton brokerage, lay in ruins in the foreground. The buildings on the right are on Milk Street and include A. L. Cutter Company and Baeder, Adamson & Company. This area had seen the fire sweep Federal, Congress, and Pearl Streets in the early morning hours of Sunday November 10, and gunpower was used to destroy many buildings on Milk, Bath, Kilby, Water, Hawes and Lindall Streets at Liberty Square to try and bank the fire.

A photograph by James Wallace Black shows men standing on the rubble of Brewer and Tileston Company which was owned by Thomas Mayo Brewer and John Boies Tileston and located at 17 Milk Street. Brewster and Tileston were well-known printers and booksellers and in the 1870s would annually print the *Old Farmer's Almanac*. The three granite piers are what remains of the building with massive granite blocks strewn in the foreground.

THE SIGHT WAS A PECULIAR ONE

The utter devastation of the Burnt District in the days after the fire was beyond comprehension. Standing on Washington Street, one could see to the waterfront with whole blocks leveled by the fire. Smoke still rose from cellar holes where wood and combustible materials lay and smolder, creating an eerie and unearthly light as the dawn broke. The *History of the Great Conflagration* states: "Huge fields of glowing ruins, covered with smoldering lambent fires, occasionally broken by piles of half-destroyed debris or standing walls, up which the blaze climbed and played, while overall hung a dense, murky pall of smoke, slowly floating to the southward in rolling, heaving billows, born by the gentle breeze."

It was surreal and Frothingham states "the whole of the sixty [five] acres were so thickly strewn with debris that he who explored the area had to clamber over granite blocks, hot piles of bricks, and stumble against the projecting ends of iron columns half buried in the mass of rubbish." That did not deter the public who descended upon the area pell-mell and a great number of who came out of either curiosity or with the intention of pilfering. With the militia called out, one could hear the "tramp, tramp of the sentinels, as they paced their lonely beasts, and the dangerous click of the gun locks as they challenged those who manifested a desire to encroach upon their domain.... Boston was literally under martial law Monday and Tuesday nights. Here and there a squad of the horse patrol dashed through the streets, in and out of the burned district, and the dark blue coats and brass buttons of the city police were omnipresent."

However, it was daunting, and Russell Conwell describes the scene:

Very little, if anything, was left to show what had been. In the stead of the noble buildings of granite and marble and brick were huge, giant walls, torn and ragged, and broken columns of stone and iron. The lines of the streets were entirely obliterated; and the ways were so blocked by great bowlders of granite, and heaps of debris,—in some places from three to ten feet deep,—that those who had been most familiar with the section before the fire were utterly unable to find their way, and groped about, or clambered over the obstructing rock, brick, iron, and still hot rubbish, dazed and bewildered.

AFTER THE FIRE, BY OLIVER WENDELL HOLMES

When far along the eastern sky I saw the flags of Havoc fly,
As if his forces would assault The sovereign of the starry vault
And hurl Him back the burning rain that seared the cities of the plain,
I read as on a crimson page the words of Israel's sceptered sage:—

For riches make them wings, and they do as an eagle fly away.

O vision of that sleepless night, what hue shall paint the mocking light
That burned and stained the orient skies where peaceful morning loves to rise, as if the
sun had lost his way and dawned to make a second day,—above how red with fiery glow,
how dark to those it woke below!

On roof and wall, on dome and spire, flashed the false jewels of the fire;
Girt with her belt of glittering panes and crowned with starry-gleaming vanes,
our northern queen in glory shone with new-born splendors not her own, and stood,
transfigured in our eyes, a victim decked for sacrifice!

The cloud still hovers overhead, and still the midnight sky is red;
As the lost wanderer strays alone to seek the place he called his own,
His devious footprints sadly tell how changed the pathways known so well;
the scene, how new! The tale, how old ere yet the ashes have grown cold!

Again, I read the words that came writ in the rubric of the flame:
Howe'er we trust to mortal things, each hath its pair of folded wings;
Though long their terrors rest unspread their fatal plumes are never shed;
At last, at last, they stretch in flight, and blot the day and blast the night!

Hope, only Hope, of all that clings around us, never spreads her wings;
Love, though he break his earthly chain, still whispers he will come again;
But Faith that soars to seek the sky shall teach our half-fledged souls to fly,
And find, beyond the smoke and flame, the cloudless azure whence they came!

Liberty Square is the junction of Kilby, Water, and Batterymarch Streets, and looking towards Kilby Street the ground floor of J. Adan Waldo Company, manufacturers of firebrick and drainpipe, survived the fire; a sign states that the company removed to No. 4 Liberty Square. Signs for several businesses can be seen on several partially standing buildings in the right foreground. On the far left of the building, two signs have been posted indicating the transferal of businesses formerly located on that site.

Soldiers armed with rifles with fixed bayonets guarded the Burnt District for weeks, as ruins and cellars were excavated to recover safes. Here on Milk Street, seen from Pearl Street, soldiers and men stand among the granite blocks that had imploded from the intensity of the heat as well as thousands of bricks among the debris. "The scene was picturesque in its very desolation. Beyond the line of bayonets lay the ash-covered ruins, with a group of blue-coated soldiers standing out in strong relief against the dull background. A long line of workmen was tugging at a huge cable destined to pull down a wall."

A man rests against a granite block in front of the ruins of Burr, Taft & Company, a dry goods store, at Franklin Street looking towards Milk Street. The entrance to the first floor remains but the building was destroyed by the fire and through the openings once can glimpse the destruction of the area. The spire of the Old South Meeting House is seen in the center distance. Notice the wood signs everywhere informing the public as to where the businesses had relocated.

The facade of what was once a streetscape of buildings survived the fire is a grim reminder of the devastation that can be wrought by a fire. Men stand on the rubble of brick and stone gazing at the openings that look onto a barren wasteland.

Looking from Franklin Street in the foreground towards Milk Street, seen just beyond the windowless wall the area was strewn with bricks, granite, cast iron columns as well as a gas pipe that protrudes from the rubble on the lower left. The spire of the Old South Meeting House can be seen in the distance as well as on the far left a wall of the Fowle & Sons Carpet Company on Washington Street.

Summer Street had been decimated by the fire with entire buildings of granite having imploded and reduced to broken granite boulders, seen on the left. This triangular four-story cornered building at Pearl and High Streets stands amid rubble with nothing to be seen in the distance. In the area of Pearl and High Streets was once concentrated the leather and shoe factories that provided much of the footwear in the country.

High Street, seen from Summer Street, had the remains of a flatiron building at the corner that was photographed by John P. Soule. Standing amongst the debris of the fire in the foreground, firemen and curious onlookers gaze in awe at the devastation. The area to the left had been completely destroyed by the fire. Reverend Henry Ward Beecher said: "Granite—it is a child of fire, and would seem to be able to defy the flames; but it seems as if it sparkles and cracks, and is destroyed,—as if it were chalk."

Within a few weeks, the cobblestone streets in the Burnt District had been cleared with many of the huge pieces of granite dumped into the area of Atlantic Avenue and used for fill. Seen here on Washington Street, a group of workmen gather around the granite blocks as scaffolding has been erected on the facade of the Fowle & Sons Carpet Company, once a prominent Foreign and American carpet warehouse. The Old South Meeting House, seen on the far left, had been saved by valiant efforts and proudly stood as a sentinel to the devastating fire.

Boston—Picturesque Scenes and Incidents was a collage of sketches by well-known artist and illustrator Paul Frenzeny that appeared in *Harper's Weekly* on December 7, 1872 and shows the highs and lows of the Great Boston Fire. In individual scenes the artist depicts *Fighting it Behind the Barricades, the Outside Aid Coming, Selling Relics, Boston Pluck, After the Struggle, Thieves and Roughs Arrested*, and *Looking at the Ruins*. Frenzeny was a French born artist that sketched for *Harper's Weekly* and many other publications such as *Frank Leslie's Illustrated Newspaper*. He was "Always respectful of the authenticity of his observations and sketches, Frenzeny is considered one of the most prolific and accurate special correspondents of his time." (*Author's collection*)

Opening Safes—The Books All Right is a sketch by Edwin Austin Abbey from *Harper's Weekly* November 30, 1872 that shows a merchant, under the watchful eyes of a military cadet on the left, is seen reviewing a ledger that was taken intact from the open safe on the right. Many safes were opened to unfortunately reveal that the contents had become ash, and because of the lingering heat, loss of important documents often occurred by opening the safes too soon. A sign says that Phoenix & Pluck have resumed business at No. 10 Water Street.

A Scene on Summer Street, near Kingston Street was etched by James E. Taylor and shows the recovery of safes from the store of Jewett & Bush, a woolen dealer. Teams of yoked oxen were used to pull the heavy loads on a low bullock cart as the horses were still affected by the epizootic. This was important as a safe of Westcott & Company had been recovered and its contents of $150,000 found undamaged from the fire.

The Resumption of Business took place on the site of Franklin's Birthplace on Milk Street in a sketch by Edwin Austin Abbey. Merchants are depicted leaning on overturned safes with the remains of the facade behind them and Milk Street littered with debris, granite blocks and a cast iron column. Reverend Phillips Brooks said: "There is little immediate destitution, for there were hardly any dwellings burnt, but thousands are thrown out of employment, and it is pitiable to see the rich men who have been reduced to poverty in a night. My poor friend Mr.____, the gentlest and best of men, is ruined in his old age. Every hour one hears of some new sufferer, but the strength and brightness of every one is amazing."

Boston Enterprise—Going it on Wheels was a sketch by James E. Taylor showing C. C. Perkins Sheepskins having created a wood shed with an office, that was on wheels and pulled by a pair of yoked oxen. Burnt out of their location at 3 Pearl Street, this was certainly a novel way of continuing in the leather business while remaining in the city, albeit on wheels. It might seem Mr. Perkins was down on his luck but he created a movable business that traversed the city streets until he could find a new permanent location. Notice the sheep hides nailed to the left of the shed.

The Association for the Relief of Unemployed Workingwomen in Session at the Park Street Church was a sketch by James E. Taylor that appeared in *Frank Leslie's Illustrated News*. Russell Conwell said: "Money being the one great need of women who are out of employment, it is gratifying to inform them that there is enough in the relief fund to meet all exigencies. This money, as we understand it, belongs to people who have been thrown out of employment. It is in no sense a charity that the applicants accept in taking money from the hands of the Relief Committee. They are simply acting in the place of their former employers, and paying them money that is as much their own as if they had worked for it with the needle, the sewing-machine, or any other implement of industry. At present, the headquarters of relief for working-women are in the basement of Park-street Church, where Mrs. William Claflin and her corps of noble-hearted women and other co-workers are to be found to attend to all who may call upon them. No girl or woman who has been thrown out of employment need be ashamed to visit these headquarters."

Families who were Burnt out Applying to the Committee for Relief was sketched by James E. Taylor and appeared in *Frank Leslie's Illustrated News*. Russell Conwell said: "For days and weeks after the great disaster, the various headquarters of relief committees were crowded with anxious seekers after employment and temporary relief. The doorways were sometimes so crowded, and the offices so full, that a ticket-system had to be adopted, by which only a certain number could be admitted at once. The overseers of the poor in the Chardon-street building, the Woman's Relief Office at the Park-street Church, the Young Men's Christian Association, the Young Women's Christian Association, the Young Men's Christian Union, City Hall, and Boffin's Bower, heard tales of distress and of patient toil at which Boston was astonished."

William L. Burt was the Post Master of Boston and he recounted: "Our mails were removed without the loss of a letter or newspaper and stored in the Customs House. I applied to the city for the use of Faneuil Hall before the fire stopped burning, and Sunday morning commenced moving to Faneuil Hall. Sunday night I advertised in the newspaper that the office would be opened as usual at Faneuil Hall at 10 o'clock. This would have been accomplished and everything as we had planned in the morning after but for the fact that the gas was cut off at one o'clock in the morning on account of the second fire and we were obliged to lay in darkness with over one hundred men until daylight losing nearly seven hours. The clerks employed in the Post Office all of them kept at Faneuil Hall had their meals there and sleeping on the floor." Members of the militia pass letters to the mailboxes on the stairs. Shortly afterwards the Old South Meeting House would be used as a temporary post office until the new post office was completed at Post Office Square in 1878.

6

THE TRIAL BY FIRE

COLUMBIA LAYS ASIDE HER LAURELS TO MOURN AT THE BURNING OF HER BIRTH-PLACE

Columbia Lays Aside Her Laurels to Mourn at the Burning of Her Birth-place was an etching that appeared in *Harper's Weekly* on November 30, 1872. This etching was by Thomas Nast, an important artist and a noted political cartoonist of the nineteenth century. This image shows *Columbia*, the female national personification of the United States, doubled over in abject grief casting aside the laurels of the national victory of Ulysses S. Grant's reelection, foreign arbitration in regards to San Juan and the Alabama Claims. A serpent coiffed devil, with a burning torch in his hand, emerges from the devastation to ascend into the sky with the smoke from Boston's inferno enveloping him and the ruins of the city. (*Author's collection*)

The Burnt District, as the 65 acres of Boston had become known, had an almost picturesque quality of the ruins with walls of brick or stone arches marking the site of once successful businesses. Hartford's *The Weekly Times* on November 16, 1872 said that the devastation was "A Sublime and Awful Sight." During the weeks following the fire, the ruins were visited by people daily "who gazed at the sad reality, and contemplated the situation, while all around them the busy gangs of men laid low the dangerous walls." Here, on the site of the H. M. Williams Company at 42 India Street, a group of men pose for a photograph, sitting among the debris of bricks, granite blocks, and iron columns that were strewn throughout the area.

John Damrell had repeatedly warned the mayor and members of the Board of Alderman that Boston was at risk of a fire and had attempted to take preventative measures by trying to improve firefighting methods which fell on deaf ears with none of the necessary funding. Though he had warned that a serious fire was imminent, Damrell was ultimately blamed for the fire. He lost his job as the city's chief fire engineer in 1874 and his position was replaced by the Board of Fire Commissioners. Damrell became the first president of the National Association of Fire Engineers and served as president of the Massachusetts State Firemen's Association, and ongoing service to the Charitable Relief Associations of the Boston Fire Department. He spent the rest of his life working to implement a national building code. He also served for many years as the commissioner of the Boston Building Department.

A Visitation Intended to Shock the Minds of Our Citizens

The reaction by ministers to the devastation wrought by the Great Fire was swift and condemning and was to be fodder for sermons for the next few months. F. E. Frothingham said that "people, instead of attending Divine service, thronged to the streets immediately about the fire, and churches were deserted." However the following Sunday ministers throughout Boston preached on the fire and its implications on life, greed, and loss. Rev. Dr. Manning of the Old South Chapel preached *The Lord gave, and the Lord hath Taken Away*, Rev. Dr. Webb of the Shawmut Congregational Church preached *Shall there be evil in a city, and the Lord hath not done it?* and Rev. John Beckley of the Somerset Street Baptist Church preached *Every man's work shall be manifest when the day shall declare it; for it shall be revealed by fire*. However it was the Rev. Cyrus Bartol of the West Church who preached *The Trial By Fire* in which he delivered a sermon that was said to be a "fine analysis of the influence of a great disaster upon the human mind, an acute essay on the harmony of nature above and beyond any local derangement of the elements; and was, withal, filled with sound, practical suggestions as to improve methods of city building, and a severe invective against the spirit of lawlessness now pervading the country. The conflagration should be considered, not merely as an accident which could be easily repaired, but as a visitation intended to shock the minds of our citizens into a due sense of the undue greed and haste which led to the building of mushroom blocks."

Within weeks, the General Relief Committee made a series of resolutions that represented the opinions of nearly every citizen of Boston. This resolution was to create a more modern city by a new urban plan.

Resolved, That the appeal to the city of Boston to establish anew in the burnt district the lines of all the streets which are too narrow or too crooked for the present and future wants of the chief city of New England, imperatively demands immediate action.

Reverend Cyrus Augustus Bartol was the minister of the West Church on Cambridge Street in Boston's West End at the time of the Great Boston Fire. He was graduated from Bowdoin College and the Harvard Divinity School and not only preached for fifty years, but was an author and would publish articles in various periodicals including the *Christian Examiner, the North American Review*, and the *Unitarian Review*. In 1849, he published *Hymns for the Sanctuary*, also known as the "West Boston Collection," and was well respected for his insightful writing. *The New York Tribune* referred to Bartol as "probably the most successful minister in Boston," and he had a wide following that respected and admired him.

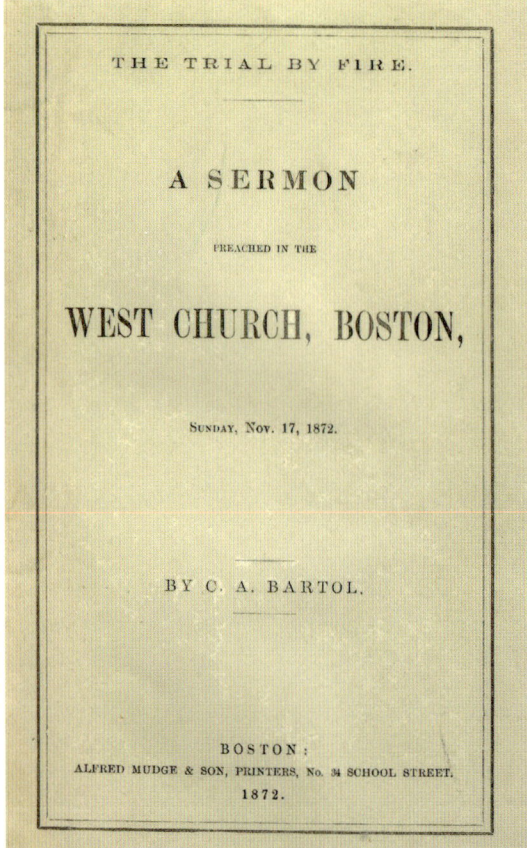

THE TRIAL BY FIRE.

A SERMON

PREACHED IN THE

WEST CHURCH, BOSTON,

SUNDAY, NOV. 17, 1872.

BY C. A. BARTOL.

BOSTON:
ALFRED MUDGE & SON, PRINTERS, No. 34 SCHOOL STREET.
1872.

On Sunday November 17, 1872 Reverend Cyrus A. Bartol preached a sermon *The Trial By Fire*, which was printed by Alfred Mudge & Sons. His sermon was both powerful and thought provoking and a quote from the moving sermon is as follows: "For our calamity is our penalty, a fine we pay long ago predicted to our inflammable architecture by prophets of combustion, yet defied by greed of rapid gain, but coming to pass as naturally in the high tinder-boxes ranged close together out of reach of engines, as when you drill a hole and put in the charge and light the fuse, or lay the train, the blast follows." (*Author's collection*)

William Lloyd Garrison, known as the "Grand Old Man of Boston," was a well-known publisher in Boston having since 1831 printed the *Liberator* as the voice piece of the abolitionist movement in Boston. He once said: "I am in earnest—I will not equivocate—I will not excuse—I will not retreat a single inch—and I will be heard" and he was for over three decades. He lived at *Rockledge*, his house at 125 Highland Street in Roxbury and a city which had been annexed to Boston in 1868, and was a well-known fire buff who took the train to Boston just after the fire. Upon his arrival he found Boston to be "a sad, wonderful, and fascinating sight to see the ruins from Washington street, extending from Summer to Milk Streets, thus sweeping broadly to the water."

Louisa May Alcott, the well-known author of *Little Women*, described the Great Boston Fire as a "Splendid and terrible sight" and with the commotion and spread of the fire she was up all night. In a letter to Anna Alcott Pratt she says: "The fire was so great that it created a whirlwind & an awful roar. I saw blazing boards, great pieces of cloth, & rolls of paper flying in all directions falling on roofs & spreading the fire. The granite blocks on Franklin St. went down like card houses, & heavy cornices peeled off as if of paper. Fire men could not go up their ladders the heat was so intense & many were killed by falling walls.... The red glare, the strange roar, the flying people, all made [the] night terrible, & I kept thinking of the Last Days of Pompeii. I enjoyed it immensely till two o'clock, & then we went home to get warm."

Dr. Oliver Wendell Holmes was a well-known writer in Boston and was the author of *The Autocrat of the Breakfast Table* which gave Boston the moniker the "Hub of the Universe." Holmes was an important medical reformer and a member of the Boston Society for Medical Improvement. In 1872 he wrote a letter to John Lothrop Motley, former Minister to Austria and Great Britain who was living in England, describing the fire: "There was no getting very near the fire; but that night and the next morning I saw it dissolve the great high buildings, which seemed to melt away in it. My son Wendell made a remark which I found quite true, that great walls would tumble and yet one would hear no crash,—they came down as if they had fallen on a vast featherbed. Perhaps, as he thought, the air was too full of noises, for us to note what would in itself have been a startling crash. I hovered around the Safety Vaults in State Street, where I had a good deal of destructible property of my own and others, but no one was allowed to enter them. So, I saw (on Saturday morning) the fire eating its way straight toward my deposits, and millions of others with them, and thought how I should like it to have them wiped out with that red flame that was coming along clearing everything before it. But I knew all was doing that could be done, and so I took it quietly enough, and managed to sleep both Saturday and Sunday night tolerably well, though I got up every now and then to see how far and how fast the flames were spreading northward."

Alexander Graham Bell was a noted educator and he provided pedagogical instruction to teachers at the Boston School for Deaf Mutes on Pemberton Square in Boston. Throughout his lifetime, Bell sought to integrate the deaf and hard of hearing with the hearing world. However, his greatest claim to fame was that he is credited with inventing and patenting the telephone. He co-founded the American Telephone and Telegraph Company in 1885. Bell was an eyewitness to the Great Boston fire and wrote: "You will have heard of poor Boston by this time. 200 acres of the best buildings burned down. I was—in common with half the male popul. of Boston out all night on Saturday. Fire broke out again today [November 11] and is now raging. More money destroyed than at Chicago. I am dead tired so will turn. I shall write you full details in the Globe newspaper."

Harvey Washington Wiley, later known as the "Father of Pure Food," was a volunteer firefighter at the Great Boston fire, joining with others as they pulled a fire engine by hand from Cambridge across the West Boston Bridge spanning the Charles River. This reminiscence appeared in his autobiography. (*Courtesy Library of Congress*)

The big fire of 1872 in Boston stands out in my memory—both because of its magnitude and because I was one of the firemen. There were no electric street-cars and of course no autos; the horse was the chief factor in transportation. It happened that an epidemic of "epizootic," or flu, attacked the horses of Boston in serious proportions. Most of the fire horses had it. The students formed companies to man the fire engines in case of necessity. The necessity arose suddenly!

About eight o'clock on Saturday evening, November 9, 1872, the fire-bells rang. The engine to which I had been assigned was directly across from my rooming-house on Church Street [in Cambridge.] In a short time, a hundred students assembled at this machine. We were told that the fire was in Boston, and we could see the glow without any difficulty. On either side of a long rope we started for Boston. We urged our engine forward with all the power we had, fearing that the fire would be put out before we got there.

We need not have worried about that. When we approached the business center we saw that this fire was not a small one. The scene at our first position near Devonshire Street was appalling and majestic. The buildings were largely of granite, with large granite pillars. As the stone became heated and the streams of water poured upon the buildings the granite disintegrated rapidly. Little by little we were crowded back but still we stood by our engines.

The supply of water was not very abundant in this locality because when it was changed from residence to business the water service had not been enlarged. Finally, Sunday afternoon as the last resort a number of houses were blown up and thus the old South Church and the new post-office were saved. It is said that the light from the conflagration was seen sixty miles inland. The Sunday trains brought thousands of visitors to the badly stricken city. Thieves became busy; extra police were appointed and the militia were brought into service. The fire was finally brought under control about four o'clock Sunday afternoon. In all about sixty-seven acres, thickly covered with buildings to the number of nearly eight hundred, were destroyed. The loss in property was estimated at nearly one hundred million dollars. This includes buildings and merchandise. There was some loss of life also but not very great. The disaster was chiefly commercial. It was estimated that Harvard College lost about forty thousand dollars 'annual income as the result of the fire. Coming at the beginning of winter it was particularly hard on the laboring people, both men and women being thrown out of employment. The people of Boston and vicinity who had not suffered in the fire raised about three hundred thousand dollars for the relief of the suffering. Chicago, which had been helped a little over a year before by generous contributions from Boston, came back with equally generous offerings of aid. After all, like the Chicago fire, the general result was helpful. It enabled Boston to straighten some very crooked streets and to install a better water service.

Colonel Russell H. Conwell was the author of *The History of the Great Fire of Boston*, which recounted the impact of the fire on the city, and was written "to place before the present generation a readable and trustworthy account of the great fire in Boston." Conwell had attended Yale and in 1862 he enlisted as captain of Company F of the 46th Massachusetts Infantry Regiment in the Civil War. He studied law at the Albany Law School, and was later ordained a Baptist minister. He is best remembered as the founder and first president of Temple University in Philadelphia. Today, Conwell's name lives on in the Gordon-Conwell Theological Seminary, an interdenominational seminary formed in 1969 by the merging of two former divinity schools, Conwell School of Theology of Temple University in Philadelphia and Gordon Divinity School.

Thomas A. Nast was a prominent political cartoonist in the nineteenth century, and he was considered to be the "Father of the American Cartoon." He was associated with the *New York Illustrated News*, *Frank Leslie's Illustrated News*, and *Harper's Weekly* and his sketches and cartoons had a wide appeal to the public. His dramatic sketch *Columbia Lays Aside Her Laurels to Mourn at the Burning of her Birth-Place* was to become a visual symbol of the submissive grief caused by the devastation.

Above left: A sixteen-page supplement to *Frank Leslie's Illustrated Newspaper* was printed recounting the Great Boston Fire in detail with an etching of the Cathedral Building engulfed in flames and both firemen and civilians grouped in the foreground. Known as the Cathedral Building as it was built on the site of the Cathedral of the Holy Cross at the corner of Franklin and Devonshire Streets, it was also where the *Boston Pilot* was printed. The fire was sketch by James E. Taylor and appeared as *A Prey to the Flames* in the November 23, 1872 Supplement to *Frank Leslie's Illustrated Newspaper.*

Above right: John Boyle O'Reilly was a member of the Irish Republican Brotherhood, then commonly known as the "Fenians", a secret society of rebels dedicated to an armed uprising against British rule. Convicted of treason he was exiled to Australia. He escaped and eventually arrived in Boston. As a journalist, writer, poet and eventually editor of the *Boston Pilot*, he was one of the most famous literary figures of his day, publishing four volumes of poetry and two novels. O'Reilly was particularly moved by the Great Boston Fire, and he wrote a poem simply titled *Boston*, questioning the role God has played in using fire to teach Bostonians a lesson:

> *O Broad-Breasted Queen among Nations! O Mother, so strong in thy youth!*
> *Has the Lord looked upon thee in ire, and willed thou be chastened by fire,*
> *Without any ruth?*
> *Has the Merciful tired of his mercy, and turned from thy sinning in wrath,*
> *That the world with raised hands sees and pities thy desolate daughters, thy cities,*
> *Despoiled on their path?*
> *One year since thy youngest was stricken: Thy eldest lies stricken to-day.*
> *Ah! God, was thy wrath without pity, to tear the strong heart from our city,*
> *And cast it away?*
> *O Father! forgive us our doubting: The stain from our weak souls efface;*
> *Thou rebukest, we know, but to chasten; thy hand has but fallen to hasten*
> *Return to thy grace.*
> *Let us rise purified from our ashes as sinners have risen who grieved;*
> *Let us show that twice-sent desolation on every true heart in the nation*
> *Has conquest achieved.*

Reverend Henry Ward Beecher, minister of the Plymouth Congregational Church in Brooklyn, New York, recounted the Boston he knew as a child that was destroyed by the fire: "I go back to my boyhood, when I lived there. I remember all the streets that have been desolated by this fire. I have run through them of errands; I have played through them. I remember the stately old residences where the old families dwelt. Little by little the streets have been given up, street after street, to business-purposes, and gorgeous stores have taken the place of the proud residences, and changes have come over the whole of this part of the city. And such stores! What solidity! what height! what capacity! It seemed as if ingenuity had concentrated in the building of them all its exercise. Architecture has done its best; and yet the flame has puffed out its lips at them, and they are gone."

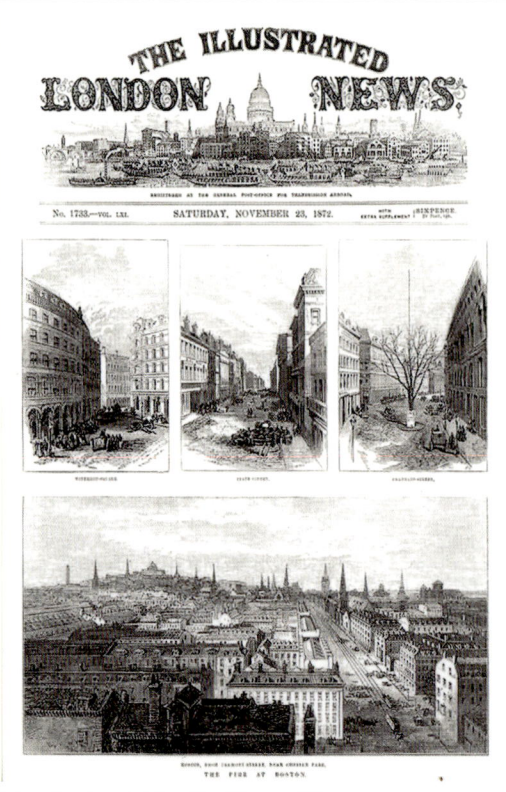

The cover of *The London Illustrated News* on November 23, 1872, which had and extra supplement, featured etchings on the Great Boston Fire showing scenes in the city before the fire. Winthrop Square, State Street, Franklin Street, and Boston from Tremont Street near Chester Park in Boston's South End (which was nowhere near the fire) were all testimony as Boston having been built up with impressive buildings in the years following the Civil War as a marvel of architecture and urban planning.

The London Illustrated News on November 23, 1872 had a full page of etchings done in the aftermath of the fire. These graphic etchings showed the ruins of a city that had once been pride of place of New England, with huge blocks of granite protruding from the debris. On the lower right is the Old South Meeting House, valiantly saved by men with wet blankets on the roof, and water sprayed from the *Amoskeag* engine thought the night.

The London Illustrated News on November 23, 1872 accurately depicted scenes of the devastation, with not just ruins in the area of the Burnt District, but also the recovering safes from the destroyed businesses and the saving of papers and mail from the post office.

William Barrett Washburn was the governor of Massachusetts in 1872, and after the fire he was instrumental in urging the legislature to be called into a special session to enable the provision of state assistance for the rebuilding of Boston. Measures passed included a bill simplifying the establishment of insurance companies, since several were bankrupted by the blaze, and a bill authorizing the city to issue bonds to speed the rebuilding effort, which would encompass sixty-five acres of Boston.

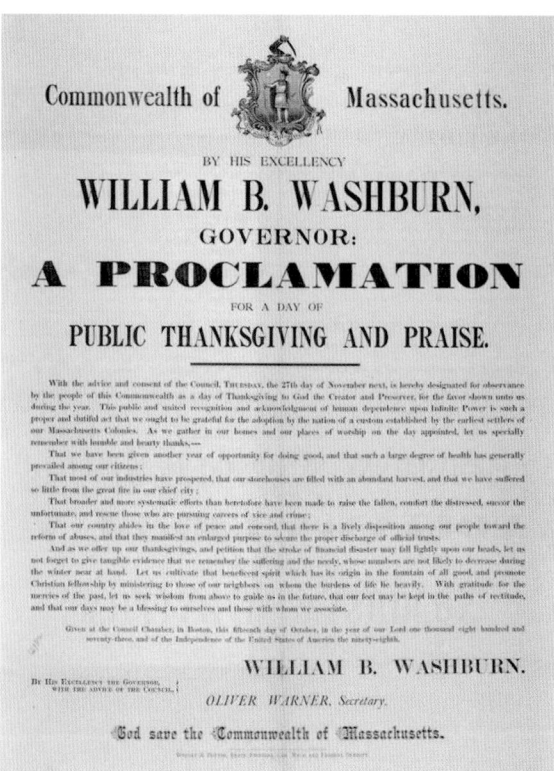

Governor Washburn, with the advice and consent of the Council, issued a *Proclamation for a Day of Public Thanksgiving and Praise* to take place on November 27, 1872 in reaction to the extreme severity of the fire in Boston. His proclamation declared a day of Thanksgiving to God the Creator and Preserver, for the favor shown unto us during the year and "That most of our industries have prospered, that our storehouses are filled with and abundant harvest, and that we have suffered so little from the great fire in our chief city; That broader and more systematic efforts than heretofore have been made to raise the fallen, comfort the distressed, succor the unfortunate, and rescue those who are pursuing careers of crime and vice."

"Homeless Tonight," or "Boston in Ashes," was a song composed by Charles Albert White which was published by White, Smith & Perry of Boston. The cover of the sheet music was printed by J. H. Bufford's Sons in 1872 and depicts two terrified young girls clinging to one another as they escape from the burning city with the tower of Trinity Church on Summer Street in flames behind them. One poignant stanza of the song was "Who will pity us, and who will give us shelter thro' this sad and lonely night." The sheet music was dedicated to William F. Chase of Suffolk Hose Company 5 of Boston.

The sheet music of "Homeless Tonight" was written after the Great Fire of November 9, 1872 by Charles A. Wright who was a well-known song writer of the period. The sheet music proved so popular that it ran through several editions, and was a piece for piano that could be played at home and thereby rekindle memories of the fire. White's lyrics created a sentimental and heartfelt pity for the two young orphans depicted on the sheet music cover:

Lone and weary thro' the streets we wander,
For we have no place to lay our heads,
Not a friend on earth is left to shelter us,
For both our parents now are dead.
Poor mother died when we were both young,
Yet father made for us a home,
But now he's killed by falling timbers,
And we are left here all alone.

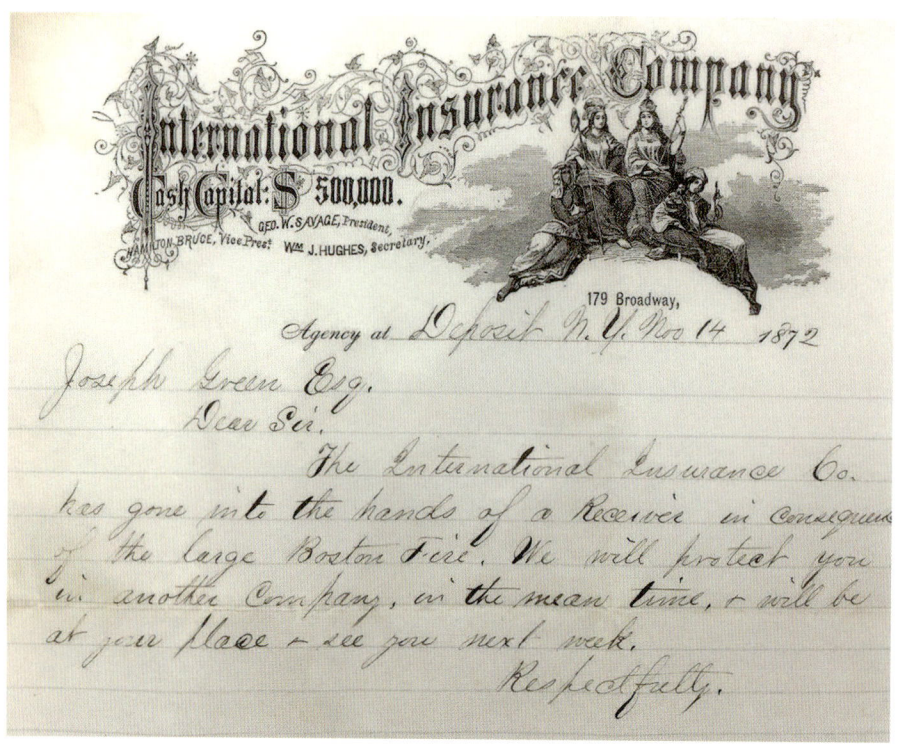

A letter to Joseph Green, Esq. from The International Insurance Company dated November 14, 1872 stated that "The International Insurance Co. has gone into the hands of a Receiver in consequence of the large Boston fire. We will protect you in another company, in the meantime, & will be at your place & see you next week." Lucius Beebe put it succinctly "The insurance companies of Massachusetts, nearly every one of which was bankrupted by the extent of the calamity, were given permission to reorganize."

A commemorative bronze medallion was struck by the Dorchester Mutual Fire Insurance Company for the seventy-fifth anniversary of the company's founding in 1855. Seen on the obverse, it depicts Currier and Ives' print of the Great Boston Fire of 1872; on the reverse it states "The only existing Boston insurance company which survived the Great 1872 Fire." Many of the local insurance companies were ruined by the tremendous insurance claims but the Dorchester Mutual Fire Insurance Company survived. Thomas French Temple was an employee, and later president of the company, and he had joined the Dorchester fire department in 1856 serving as clerk and foreman of Engine 1; foreman of Engine 5 at Neponset, and held that office when Steam Fire Engine 20 was introduced, being in command of the company at the time of the big fire in 1872. (*Author's collection*)

7

SPRINGING PHOENIX-LIKE FROM THE ASHES

Church Green is the junction of Bedford and Summer Streets, and was rebuilt after the fire with five-
and six-story commercial buildings that created an impressive streetscape, along with interesting
signage, in the 1870s. In this vein, Rev. Cyrus Bartol said: "Boston admires Boston; she is worthy the
admiration she wins from those she bore not, in her borders or far away. She gets up quick from her
fall, rubs her robes, professes she is not hurt, makes nobly light of and laughs at her hoist to the ground;
she says she is no beggar, and wants to refuse the alms, like a prince she has bestowed; a grand temper
not unbecoming, but to be prized as one of the pillars of virtue."

Looking west on Summer Street from where the fire had started on November 9, 1872, the area was completely rebuilt by 1876. Seen in the center, the spire of the Park Street Church, designed by Peter Banner and built in 1809, towers above the intersection of Summer, Washington and Winter Streets. With buildings that had shops on the ground floor and manufactories, small factories and offices on the upper floors, this was to become a thriving mercantile and commercial district and where numerous department stores were to be located.

Washington Street, looking north from Winter Street, was dominated by the Old South Meeting House, a landmark of Boston which was valiantly saved by firemen from New Hampshire with the *Amoskeag* engine. The buildings on the right, stretching from Summer to Milk Street, were built between 1873 and 1876 and had a variety of shops, commercial concerns and department stores. Notice Raymond's in the center, a popular department store that had 'Unkle Eph' as the store spokesperson who touted "Yankee common sense" with reasonable prices. The ease of access by streetcar, seen in the center, meant that not only shoppers by also employees working in the area could conveniently travel from all parts of the city to get here.

Springing Phoenix-like from the Ashes

The devastation of the fire was tremendous, and was a shock not just to Bostonians, but to the readers of national newspapers. *The New York Tribune* had reporters and correspondents sending information for the daily news, as well as artists who sketched the ruins. The newspapers "printed thousands of words of dispatches, including an hour by hour account of the progress of the blaze, a complete list of the destroyed properties, maps of the Boston business district, the assets and Boston liabilities of scores of insurance companies, stories on the local angle of the calamity and other features which many might imagine the devising only of recent high-pressure reporting." Day after day new stories were printed including that in the *New York Times* on November 13, 1872 that boldly declared "Boston Alive Again" and that "Business Men Too Busy to Mourn Over Their Losses." Indeed, the regrouping and Yankee pluck was more than evident as businesses relocated and began anew.

Frank E. Frothingham said in his book *The Boston Fire* that many merchants "commenced the erection of temporary buildings, some on the ruins of their warehouses, and on the site of Fort Hill. Washington Square, in this locality, was soon covered with buildings of corrugated iron, and occupied by boot, shoe, leather and iron dealers. The dispersion of trade carried the various branches of business into strange localities" and spread commerce near and far. Businesses would rebuild but the city of Boston oversaw the progress by appointing a city architect. The first was George C. Clough and he was now responsible for new buildings erected in Boston. Clough had once been with Snell and Gregerson, and was an independent architect when the city appointed him to oversee not just the rebuilding of the New Boston on the ruins of the Burnt District, but he also designed numerous schools for the City of Boston, several local churches, and many other municipal buildings and public charitable institutions throughout the Boston area.

As Lucius Beebe said: "The guilty Mansard roof was banished in perpetuity and the florid cornices ... were less in vogue. More capacious water mains and frequent and improved hydrants promised a more suitable supply of water in the event of future emergencies. In two years all sign of the conflagration had disappeared and in a slightly longer period the ministers of the town and its leading after-dinner speakers had even wearied of the once compelling phrase 'springing Phoenix-like from the ashes.'"

The stretch of Washington Street from School to State Street was known as Cornhill, and seen in this photograph was dominated by skyscrapers that created an urbane and densely developed city. On the left was the *Herald Traveler*, and on the right the *Boston Globe*, two of the leading newspapers in New England. On the far right is the Old South Building, designed by Arthur Bowditch and built in 1903.

Milk Street was rebuilt after the fire with impressive buildings, some with white marble facades. The building in the center between the two white marble façade buildings was built on the site of the birthplace of Benjamin Franklin and was called the Franklin Building. A bust of Franklin, within a hooded niche, is perched above the entrance. The bunting and flags adorning the facades was to celebrate the 100th anniversary of the United States in 1876. Notice the Centennial Lunch Room, seen of the left, also named for the centennial festivities.

Looking east on Milk Street, the area had been built up with impressive buildings that led to the new Post Office Square, a large open area in front of the U.S. post office and sub-treasury. In the distance can be seen the spire of the Mutual Life Insurance Company of New York.

The U.S. post office and sub-treasury was designed Alfred A. Mullet, in association with Gridley J. Fox Bryant and Alexander R. Esty, and was in the process of being built when the fire destroyed the surrounding area. It was the most impressive building built during the Victorian period and was in the Renaissance style and built of granite. On the tops of the two towers flanking the center roof were two 17-foot-high white marble statues by Daniel Chester French. On the left was "Labor," supporting domestic life and sustaining the fine arts, and on the right "Science," which was controlling the forces of the new-fangled electricity and steam. The central portion was ornamented with a heraldic figure, which was appropriately an eagle with outspread wings grasping a shield with its talons. The building was demolished in 1929 and new granite Art Deco post office, designed by Cram and Ferguson, was featured upon its completion in the September 1933 issue of *Architectural Forum* magazine devoted to "The Planning of Public Buildings." The building was renamed in 1972 the John W. McCormack Post Office and Court House in honor of U.S. Congressman John W. McCormack.

The Equitable Building of the Equitable Life Assurance Society was designed by Arthur Gilman and built in 1874 at the corner of Devonshire and Milk Streets. Founded in 1859, the society was one of the largest life insurance companies in the country. On the roof was located the Boston Time Ball, a metal ball which was 4 feet in diameter and made of rolled plate copper. It was raised on a staff 20 feet high giving a clear 16-foot drop. A brake mechanism was used to stop the ball after it had dropped to within 6 feet of the bottom. Much like the Greenwich, England Observatory that since 1833 has a ball that still drops at 1:00 p.m. daily, the Boston Time Ball was an important way to verify the setting of the marine chronometers of ships in the nearby harbor. Not just were they used for celestial navigation, but being on such a tall building at Post Office Square it could be seen by both pedestrians as well as those on ships in Boston Harbor.

At 11:55 a.m. the ball is to be at half-mast.
At 11:58 a.m. the ball is to be at the top of the mast.
At 12h 0m 0s noon (Boston State House time) the ball will fall.

The Mutual Life Insurance Company of New York, with its prominent 234-foot four-sided clock tower, was designed by Peabody and Stearns and built in 1875. The New England Mutual Life Insurance Company on the right was designed by Nathaniel J. Bradlee and built in 1874. The two buildings, though designed by two separate architects, were uniquely complimentary and built of white marble with Renaissance Revival details and embellishments. The impressive duplex building dominated the south flank of Post Office Square until its demolition in 1945. It is now the site of the Post Office Square Parking Garage.